Simplify:
Eliminate Stress and Fatigue through Simple Living

Donna J. Davis

Donna J. Davis
DJD Communications, LLC
8325 S Via Del Palacio

djdcommunications@gmail.com
http://DonnaJDavis.com

Limits of Liability and Disclaimer of Warranty

The author and publisher shall not be liable for your misuse of this material. This book is strictly for informational and educational purposes.

Warning – Disclaimer

The purpose of this book is to educate and entertain. The author and/or publisher do not guarantee that anyone following these techniques, suggestions, tips, ideas, or strategies will become successful. The author and/or publisher shall have neither liability nor responsibility to anyone with respect to any loss or damage caused, or alleged to be caused, directly or indirectly by the information contained in this book.

What's causing you the most stress?
Are you your own worst enemy?

Download the "Stress Management-Self Care Worksheet" plus
learn how to "Stop these 7 Self-Defeating Habits Now."

Go to http://DonnaJDavis.com/freebies
for your bonus reports.

Contents

Dedicated to
All those who have struggled with
fatigue, overwhelm, excessive stress,
and endless demands, and have chosen
a different path.

How Do I Get There From Here?

"To find the universal elements enough; to find the air and the water exhilarating; to be refreshed by a morning walk or an evening saunter... to be thrilled by the stars at night; to be elated over a bird's nest or a wildflower in spring - these are some of the rewards of the simple life." ~John Burroughs

There was a tourist from a big city who wanted to get to a relative's home in an obscure coastal New England town. After driving around for what seemed like hours, he finally saw a local farmer and asked him how to get to this town. The farmer rubbed his chin, thought for several minutes, looked around at the possible routes, and finally told the tourist, "You can't get there from here."

While that story makes us smile, sometimes it feels true. If you look at your life right now with all the stress, overwhelm, and fatigue, the dream of living a simple life might very well seem like "you can't get there from here."

The good news is: You can!

Let's start with where you are today. Do you wake up in the middle of the night with your heart pounding because you can't remember if you emailed your business partner the proposal with the one final (and very important) change for today's presentation? You have so many responsibilities, the stress is strangling you.

You used to be great at multi-tasking. Now it seems to be taking all your energy to stay focused on finishing that last piece of your company's budget. Your fatigue is getting worse every day.

Your car broke down and you needed to pay for the repairs on your credit card. You can't get to sleep at night wondering how you are going to pay for yet another bill. No matter how hard you work, you can't seem to get on top of your finances.

You love your home and yet you can't count how many times you have lost your keys or the receipt you need to return the pair of jeans that didn't fit right. Stacks of paper and junk mail are everywhere. The clutter is overwhelming.

Oh, and on top of everything else, you volunteered to coordinate refreshments for all of your daughter's soccer practices, and you don't even know how that happened! You don't have the time to do the things you want to do for your family. And you desperately need some time to relax and to recharge your own batteries.

Life has gotten out of control and you just can't find the time to do all the things that everyone expects from you. You feel exhausted, overwhelmed, and guilty. Today is the day that you need to put an end to this madness and find some real answers.

You long for a simpler life, but you don't know where to start, and the entire process feels like one more task to be added to your "To-Do" list. You want to live more simply. You are done with the constant stress and never having enough time or energy.

This book is exactly what you need to get started simplifying your life today! We teach you the secrets for making long-lasting changes (without needing to take a year sabbatical, and without adding another two hours to your already busy day). You will learn how to begin simplifying from the inside out.

"Simplify. Simplify." ~Henry David Thoreau

To truly simplify your life, you must live in congruity with who you truly are, what you value, and what you are here to do. You must set boundaries and focus on those things and people that are the most important to you. When you are not in alignment with what's in your heart, fatigue, overwhelm, and stress flood in and take control of your life, and you get stuck running faster and faster like a hamster on a wheel.

With the fast-paced lives we live, most of us sacrifice what's important to us in order to pay the bills and to get along with others. So we'll show you how to start living the life you want by reconnecting with what you truly value, doing work you love, focusing on your priorities, getting the support you need, and having fun again.

Once you begin to make some simple shifts and changes internally, your outer life begins to shift and change as well. So, if your ultimate goal is to have a simpler, more fulfilling, and happier life, then making internal shifts can have a profound ripple effect. The results can include releasing a lot of stress, sleeping better, having the time and energy to do something fun, and being aware of the precious moments you feel you've been missing for years.

From RUST to STRUT

In the chapters of this book, we lay out ideas that you can easily incorporate into your day to begin clearing out the old to make way for the new. Each chapter starts with a reality check called:

Real-Life RUST *(Routines that Undermine Simple living Techniques)*

We identify some RUST that can make it very difficult to move toward a simple life. Then a few key points on how to begin changing the RUST are listed to summarize the info in the chapter.

The inner work we discuss will help you to sweep away the debris of negative thoughts, guilt over past mistakes, and sorrow over past regrets to get rid of the clutter in your mind.

We also offer ideas on how you can ask for help and build a support system so you don't feel alone and helpless.

If you have a mountain of responsibilities, we show you how to draw boundaries with family, colleagues, and clients. That way, you can have a high-quality life at home and professionally without stretching yourself too thin.

We encourage you to say "no" without feeling guilty that you're being selfish. We nudge you to create a schedule or to find easy ways to release some of your crazy control issues. You will learn how to delegate all sorts of tasks to free up time for the things that matter to you.

We offer tips and ideas to tackle your debt so it doesn't control so many of your choices. We tap into the latest tools and methods provided by technology to keep track of your spending (no complex Excel sheets required) and to find new ways of raising money for your business or even for your next creative project.

You will learn how to trust yourself, to slow down, and make time to listen to the voice within. You may even find yourself trusting your inner compass so much that you'll be willing to embrace the unknown, let go of expectation, and be open to far more potential and opportunity than you had ever dreamed of.

When you learn to appreciate simple joys that are all around you, you'll see the power of gratitude. You can fill your life with so much happiness that you feel the abundance of the Universe flowing into your life. (This is an amazing feeling!)

We assist you in letting the inner child run free again so that you can rediscover how to have fun again -- to regain your sense of wonder and delight that you had lost so long ago.

"Today's STRUT *(Simple Tips for your Remarkable Unique Transformation)*" suggestions end each chapter to gently push you to take a step forward. If you start implementing these action steps and become aware of what's happening inside, your life will shift. The simple life you dream of will begin to blossom.

Stress, overwhelm, and fatigue do not have to be your constant companions. We applaud you for inviting greater joy and simplicity into your life. Congratulations for stepping up to the plate!

Can you see that light at the end of the tunnel? You no longer have to live with being tired, overworked, and in constant stress. You are energized and ready to live an adventurous and brilliant life -- a life of your own design.

Yes, you can get there from here! Let's get started.

****

Have you identified what causes you the most stress?

Download your "Stress Management-Self Care Worksheet" plus learn how to "Stop these 7 Self-Defeating Habits Now" at *http://DonnaJDavis.com/freebies*

What Do I Want My Life to Look Like?

Real-Life RUST *(Routines that Undermine Simple living Techniques)*
- You doubt if you can really simplify your life. You've tried several things before and they just didn't work.
- You need time for yourself. You are at your breaking point and you don't know how to change.
- You need more money in order to live a simpler life.

Simplify by:
- Identifying what you (not anyone else) truly want for your life.
- Begin creating the life you want with baby steps. Many of these ideas you can think about while driving or getting ready in the morning.

"When you do nothing, you feel overwhelmed and powerless. But when you get involved, you feel the sense of hope and accomplishment that comes from knowing you are working to make things better." ~Author Unknown

Have you heard the saying "Your outer world is a reflection of your inner world"? Whatever is going on in your life, it first started with prolonged or repeated thoughts or feelings. If you are new to this concept, here are some common examples of outer challenges. At first, it may seem that there is no relationship between the outer and the inner workings, but let's scratch beneath the surface and explore the inter-connection.

Outer challenge: You've been turned down for a promotion at work, despite putting in long hours and your best efforts. It seems that all you do is work and now you weren't given that promised promotion.

What's happening within: You inwardly question your ability and competence to take on more responsibilities. Maybe you're torn between taking on more responsibilities at work, and spending more time at home with your family. You grew up *feeling you were never good enough.*

Outer challenge: You've achieved success in your career, but the rewards of being at the top no longer feel the same. You question whether you're willing to continue paying the price of high stress and long hours.

What's happening within: In pursuing your achievement, you may have squashed inner impulses, such as an urge to paint. When you were younger, you were *unwilling to spend the time honoring the calling of your soul*, because it didn't feel "practical." Those dreams never went away and now they are tugging harder and harder.

Outer challenge: Your environments at home and at work are disorganized and chaotic. Your schedule is jam-packed with appointments and activities. You are not moving forward professionally, and yet you feel guilty because you aren't spending enough quality time with your daughter.

What's happening within: You are *not clear on your priorities.* Your mental space is crowded with other people's opinions and attitudes of what you should be doing.
So if you work exclusively on de-cluttering your home and office, and you don't take the time to do the inner work, your wonderfully organized home will eventually end up in disarray again within a few short months. The inner work isn't really optional!

Living Life on Your Own Terms

So what if you knew there was a huge, fun world waiting for you once you begin to live life on your own terms? What if you could awaken your wildest dreams? What if you had the energy to become twice as productive and enjoy waking up each morning?

Take a few minutes and think about how you would feel when...

- You create your life, rather than reacting to it
- You enjoy every minute of the journey, not just the destination
- You choose the paths to take because they resonate with you, not because someone with a louder and stronger opinion is forcing you to
- You live a life filled with meaning and happiness and your joy spills over to the people around you
- You're not a speck of sand on the beach -- you make a difference
- You know you are a unique, magnificent being

We are all interconnected and every change you make in your inner world impacts your outer world and the worlds of those around you.

You're the Change You've Been Waiting For

Remember this phrase, "Be the change you wish to see in the world." This is commonly attributed to Gandhi, and while it is seemingly part of a bigger quote, it does urge that the initiative to change must begin with us -- from within.

You may be saying, "This is all well and good, but I have bills I cannot pay, and my kids are driving me crazy!" Maybe you have given and given to others and neglected yourself. Have you ever said, "I'm tired of being the caregiver, of being overworked, and I'm way too tired to find love."

The way ahead is not difficult, but it requires a shift in your focus. Some work and commitment on your part are necessary to create a life you love. In order to make space for the new to come into your life, you have to first decide that you are worth it. You need to make room for the shift to happen – both inside and outside.

Hans Hofmann said, *"The ability to simplify means to eliminate the unnecessary so that the necessary may speak."* To do this, you need to be clear on what's "necessary" in your life.

When we talk about simplifying our outer life, it's easy to compare it to a closet. Let's say your closet is stuffed full of clothes you hardly wear. You just purchased two beautiful light jackets and a spring dress, but you don't have anywhere to hang them! It only stands to reason that you'll have to rearrange or donate some of the old clothes to make room for the new, fun and colorful items.

The same concept applies to the work needed for clearing your inner landscape. You'll have to clear out old thinking that no longer serves you to make room for the new thoughts and the new life experiences that you desire. You must get back to basics so you can build a stronger foundation that's connected to your deepest passions and your highest hopes.

In other words, you simplify first, in order to get ahead.

If you're feeling overwhelmed, you must simplify by eliminating some tasks or commitments.

If you're wrapped up in anxieties over finding a new relationship, a career, or the meaning for your life, you must simplify by clarifying your values.

If you desire more balance or more fun in your life, simplify and evaluate what's important to you.

Here's the good news. If you don't know where to start, don't worry. We'll give you simple, clear STRUT action steps and affirmations to help you with every one of our Simple Living Secrets.

It's Never Too Late to Simplify

You may think you're too old, too busy, too (fill in the blank) to change. Yes, you may be over 30 and you may have your schedule filled with dozens of tasks. If you are completely honest with yourself though, those excuses are really because you are resisting change, no matter how unhappy you are right now. (That's normal, by the way.)

If you could see yourself in any of the earlier examples, the challenge before you is to feel worthy enough to start giving back to yourself, so you can be there for those you love.

Are you willing to take the first step in releasing your stress and overwhelm? Or do you want to cling on to years of habits just because they feel comfortable, like an old pair of slippers? Do you give into peer pressure, or do you boldly strike out on your own?

"Take the first step in faith. You don't have to see the whole staircase, just take the first step." ~ Martin Luther King, Jr.

There's so much more you want to do with your life but you're lacking the confidence and the courage to take the necessary steps. So you continue complaining about how life would be better if you had more money. You go to sleep imagining the worst-case scenarios and allow your fears to slip into conversations. You get stuck thinking that there is just no way for you to move forward.

All of those actions or thoughts are RUST and just end up aggravating the problem.

How about harnessing all the energy you're directing into fear and worry into positive life-changing action? The sooner you make the change, the sooner your life perks up and you feel happier.

It all begins with a thought and one decision…"I am willing to learn how to change." Take a deep breath and repeat that again…"I am willing to learn how to change." When you are, you have begun simplifying your life – even if you can't yet feel the change, it's begun.

"Whatever you decide, don't let it be because you don't think you have a choice." ~Hannah Harrington, Saving June

So What's Your Legacy?

Imagine that your life is the subject of a book written by a world-class writer, someone of the caliber of JK Rowling, author of the Harry Potter series. There's always a summary of the book on the inside page of the front cover. What would you like the summary of your life to say?

What adjectives would you like JK Rowling to use to describe you? How would you like to be remembered? Passionate, motivated, happy, adventurous, loving, or fulfilled? Don't focus on how you have been feeling. Focus on the feelings you want to nurture. It's all inside you. Let's get started!

Today's STRUT
(Simple Tips for your Remarkable Unique Transformation)

What Do I Want My Life to Look Like?

One of the first steps to design the life you dream of is to create a Vision Board. This is a visual representation of what you would like to attract into your life.

1. A Vision Board can be created on your computer, but it's really fun to create a tangible Vision Board. There's something therapeutic and fun about creating a Vision Board that you can post in a special place in your home. You can use a poster board, a large piece of art-paper, or even a whole wall in your study.

2. Look through magazines and books and tear out words, phrases, and pictures that speak to you. Start by writing out or finding letters that spell out "SIMPLIFY" and "MY LIFE." You may think you know what you want in your life, but for this exercise, follow the whispers of your heart. Select images that you are drawn to, even if they don't make any sense. You will begin to let your inner voice and dreams speak.

3. Cut your clippings into shapes and arrange the words and phrases around the board.

4. When you've reached a point where you feel that the pictures you chose and placed on your board depict your ideal simplified life, take a step back.

5. Are there any themes that recur throughout your pictures? Are there items on there that were a surprise?

Take the time to complete your board. Don't rush. None of the exercises in this book are meant to put any pressure on you. Give yourself whatever time you need until it you feel it reflects the life you want. With that said, please make a commitment to yourself to work through the simple exercises in this book. If you don't want to have a heart attack in the next year, your mental and physical health depend on the changes you are about to make.

Once your Vision Board is completed, look at it frequently. By impressing the pictures and themes on your subconscious, it will keep you connected to what you really want and you'll start attracting that into your life. Once you start doing your inner work, all sorts of "coincidences" start to happen. You will begin to see symbols and signs of your dreams and desires more frequently. That's when the change happens and life opens up to you. Trust the process.

Affirmations:

I have taken the first step to simplify my life.
I am gentle with myself as I take steps forward to change my life.
I deserve goodness and abundance in my life.
I find joy and happiness every day.
My life is getting better and better.

What Are Your Core Values?

Real-Life RUST
(Routines that Undermine Simple living Techniques)
- You get up, go to work, come home, fall asleep, and do it all over again tomorrow.
- You do what others think you should be doing.
- Who has time for dreams? You have bills to pay!

Simplify by:
- Identifying your core values
- Beginning to say "no" to anything and everything that doesn't match those values

"Getting in touch with your true self must be your first priority."
~Tom Hopkins

What are your core values? You may have heard of the term core values but are not quite sure what it means to you. You've heard it defined as qualities and principles that you treasure and hold most dear. That may sound a bit airy-fairy and ephemeral, but have you ever thought about why you do what you do and what really matters to you? If you haven't, then someone else or something else is steering your life.

Neale Donald Walsch, best-selling author of "Conversations with God," wrote in a blog, "As I look at life on our planet presently it feels to me that 98% of the world's people are spending 98% of their time on things that don't matter."

Where do you fall? Are you one of the 98%, or do you belong in the 2% living a life that matters, a life of greatness and magnificence where your days are filled with purpose and meaning?

Keith followed the typical career path. He finished high school, graduated with an economics degree and secured a job at his local bank. He was following in the path of his father and his uncle. Although he achieved success, he was really unhappy. It was hard for Keith to be this completely honest with himself, but he was beginning to feel that his life wasn't amounting to much. He couldn't bear the thought of living and working like this for the next 30 years until retirement.

He came across a core values worksheet online and identified with three values. His highest values were adventure, freedom, and inspiration. Given those priorities, it is no wonder that he was unhappy stuck behind a desk, working from 9 to 5 and dealing with routine duties. Keith was like a bird with his wings clipped.

Once he discovered the qualities that really motivated him and made him feel truly alive, he explored the possibilities of working in travel. He was drawn to be a hands-on travel guide. He found GA Adventures, a company that branded itself as the world's leader in adventure travel. He landed a job there as a tour leader which allowed him to live abroad for 18 months at a time.

As CEO (or Chief Experience Officer, in the language of the company's culture), Keith ended up leading very small groups on custom-designed exotic trips that styled themselves on being unforgettable and life-changing. Not your regular "tan and read while lying on the beach" type of travel.

Being the primary point person and leader for the travelers, Keith had to improvise to find solutions to any problems that arose in those foreign surroundings. Whether he was dealing with overly tired clients on the climb up to Machu Picchu or fighting off plate-sized mosquitoes on the Amazon River, he was having the time of his life.

He was no longer stuck within four walls. His backpack was his office. He was living adventure and being paid for the freedom to explore. He was fascinated with the local cultures and landscapes he was immersed in. Plus he was thrilled that his clients were inspired by this kind of adventure travel which pushed them to step outside their comfort zone and take on more risks. His new work fulfilled his core values of adventure, freedom, and inspiration.

Keith's core values are unique to him. Someone who values safety, consistency, and dependability would be totally unhappy holding Keith's job in adventure travel, but would probably thrive in a predictable office environment.

Your core values may mean little to someone else. You may share some core values with members of your church or faith community, but your priorities and your ranking of your values will most likely be different.

Shine the Light on Your Core Values

Core values shape the actions you take on a daily basis, or in challenging situations when important decisions have to be made. They define the purpose of your life and the mission you set out to fulfill. When you think about them or try to describe them, something clicks in your body. You may even feel teary because of the emotions that bubble up.

"Decide what you want, decide what you are willing to exchange for it. Establish your priorities and go to work." ~H.L. Hunt

How do you go about finding or articulating what your core values are?

When you don't act or live according to your core values, you feel disconnected, life loses its luster and you feel unmoored, like a boat adrift in the currents. There's no purpose and you become shaped by the people around you, your environment and the circumstances that befall you.

Ask yourself, "What are the two or three qualities that I must have in my life?" Without these you would feel that something isn't complete; as if you don't have enough air to breathe?

Once you initially identify these qualities, confirm that these are values that matter. When you act and live according to these qualities, you are energized, positive and motivated. You feel happy and radiate joy, as if you were plugged into an endless source of energy. You grow and you unfold. Sure, you'll have bad days (who doesn't?) but you'll bounce back quickly because there's so much that life has to offer you.

Core values are such things as adventure, accomplishment, intellectual recognition, job security, faith, stability of relationships, wealth, service to others, creativity, independence, financial freedom, fairness, justice, joy, love, and respect.

Self-help author, blogger, speaker and entrepreneur Steve Pavlina identifies nearly 500 of them in his blog http://www.stevepavlina.com/articles/list-of-values.htm. Use this as a guide to kick-start your own search, but do not adopt a core value just because it's on the list.

You are your own pilot, and this is an extremely personal process to find out more about how you're going to live the rest of your life, where you need to make changes for the better, and then how you're going about it. Don't settle for less.

Here are few things to bear in mind about core values:

- Core values will change with time and experience. When you're younger, you may place a higher value on status, fame and recognition. When you're older, you may give a higher priority to service, compassion, and legacy.

- It takes courage to live according to your core values. It's by unmasking your core values, separating them from something that's conditioned into you by family or culture, that you come into your own self and live your own purpose. Making such a bold step may upset the apple cart and disrupt the routines and lifestyles of people around you. You may choose to shift slowly or break cleanly, but if you settle for less than living a life aligned with your core values, you're simply short-changing yourself--no one else.

- You become a model of inspiration. Have you ever looked up to a successful entrepreneur, a best-selling author, or a mentor and wondered how he or she lifted themselves up from an ordinary life to one of greatness? Maybe, it's because their stars were aligned at the right time and place. Maybe they caught a few lucky breaks. More than likely though, they did the inner work we talk about here and they aligned themselves to their priorities and values. You too can live a life of magnificence. It may not be under the spotlights, but when your life is so attuned to what means most to you, you become a shining light to others.

- None of us know how many hours of life we have when we are born. We do know that time, once gone, cannot be retrieved or recycled. Time is our most precious asset. It's the currency we are given to make our mark in the world – to improve it and to leave a legacy behind for the ones who follow. Your core values ensure that you don't fritter the time away or get distracted by other things. They give you focus to concentrate your time and energy in those areas that will make the biggest positive impact on your life. They help you make better choices and they steer you towards rewarding goals and experiences.

Living Your Life in Alignment

When you embark on a journey of self-discovery and identify your core values, you may end up with a list of 10 values like this:

Love
Intimacy
Connection
Security
Legacy
Comfort
Peace

Harmony
Collaboration
Community

You can tell a lot about a person and the kind of life she lives from this list. This is a person who treasures family. She is likely an active contributor or volunteer in the local community and probably has never lived anywhere else other than the town of her birth.

This person will be happiest helping others. If offered a choice between being a social counselor or a marketing executive for a global food company, she will likely pick the former. The latter will take the person too far away from her roots.

However, let's take another set of values:

Status
Recognition
Achievement
Financial Independence
Determination
Travel
Adventure
Friendships
Connection
Intimacy

This is a person focused on being successful and getting recognized for her accomplishments. Forging ahead comes first and more than likely this person will marry late or never settle down. Remember, once the person gets all the status and financial independence she needs, the values are likely to change, but at this point in time, she will put her career ahead of getting together with friends and family.

When you start to identify your core values, you may find it challenging to narrow the values down to a handful, and then rank them in order of importance.

To make this process easier, for now, narrow down your list to your top five. Let's use the first list of 10 above. So you have love, intimacy, connection, security, and legacy. Next ask yourself, "Is connection more important than love?" "Is connection more important than intimacy?" "Is connection more important than security?" and finally "Is connection more important than legacy?" Go through this exercise with each of those five. You may find that security was actually more important to you than connection and it moves up on your scale.

This is your list. This is something that you can ponder as you're driving to work or to your client's office. There are no right or wrong answers or correct order.

Be gentle on yourself. You may have to walk away from your list as old emotions get stirred up. You may reminisce on lost opportunities and beat yourself up for making wrong choices and for wasting precious time. By taking a breather, you can relegate those emotions to where they belong – in the past. Right now, you're dealing with the rest of your life, determining how to live out the rest fully and vibrantly.

The rewards of living in alignment are truly great. When you know that *connection* and *intimacy* are more important to you than *accomplishments*, you become more confident in saying "no" to a job promotion that leaves you little time to develop meaningful relationships outside of work.

If we all lived fully aligned, without room for frustration, desperation, anger or depression, our joy would spill over and infect those around us, and our lives would be so high-wattage that we would shine to the ends of the universe.

Just Be

There's a lot of pressure on all of us to "do" and to "succeed." It is perfectly okay to take action, especially if it's action inspired by your goals and priorities. A simpler and happier life is not about doing for the sake of doing, or taking action because there are so many items left on our To-Do list. It requires that you build in time to just be -- to be in a state of awareness, to hang out with your friends, your pets, and with yourself.

At the start of a new year, in a new job or in a new relationship, we expect a lot of ourselves – to be the best performer on the job, to be the most exciting, romantic partner, or to be 10 pounds slimmer, to make new friends, to volunteer and give back and to be the best possible parent. Yes, we are reminded to lead purposeful lives and we're determined to be successful at it.

Slow down. While living meaningfully means living in accordance to values and priorities, it's okay to slack off now and again. And draw pleasure and joy from being who you are and where you are.

Music may enhance your sense of well-being. It can lift your spirit and significantly shift your mood.

Perhaps a daily walk in the park restores your connection to all life and reinforces the sense that we're all interconnected.

Playing with your dog restores your love of play and reminds you to relax.

Taking a ride on your bike and letting the wind blow through your hair nurtures your free spirit.

It's in times like these, when we give ourselves permission to relish the moment and to draw towards joy and pleasure, that we gain further insights into who we are. We find the "a-ha" moment that offers the solution to a perplexing problem, or we have time to remember to give thanks for what we have.

You can continue moving in the direction of your dreams. Goals and intentions are good and they move us forward. Working on your goals is deepened when you are being wholly grateful and thankful for who you are, and everything you have at this moment in time. The world is an enchanted place when you breathe and be.

Today's STRUT
(Simple Tips for your Remarkable Unique Transformation)

How Do I Start Being True to Myself?

1. Grab a cup of tea and a notepad. Start writing down a list of values. Don't worry about the order for now. Just write. You can use the resource listed above or simply write down feelings that you know are important to you.

2. Whittle that list down to ten. Delete the ones that sound similar, i.e., stability and consistency, performance and results. Further, narrow the list to five by using the questions included above to determine those that are most significant to you. When those seem to resonate with you, rank them in order of importance to you.
3.
4. Start being aware of the decisions you make and if they are in alignment with these values. If the decision does not match with one of your values, stop and evaluate if that is the best choice for you at this time.

Affirmations:

I make all the right choices for the life of my dreams.
I answer "yes" to the call of my soul.
I embrace and derive joy from just being.
I am aware of my core values and make decisions based on what is important to me.

Responsibilities and Boundaries

Real-Life RUST
(Routines that Undermine Simple living Techniques)

- Your family always comes first before your needs. .
- You promised the school you would be in charge of the fundraiser. Even though you really don't want to do that, you made a promise.

Simplify by:
- Saying "no" when you don't want to do something that's asked of you.
- Taking responsibility for your own actions, decisions, and work.

"Nothing is as real as a dream. The world can change around you, but your dream will not. Responsibilities need not erase it. Duties need not obscure it. Because the dream is within you, no one can take it away." ~Tom Clancy

Are you living a life that is written by others, rather than one scripted by you? Are you the breadwinner, the caregiver, the single parent who makes people-pleasing choices for the benefit of everyone else except yourself? Do you feel that you will let your family down or disappoint your friends if you don't do what they expect of you?

Rebecca feels bogged down by a never-ending list of obligations to others. She is starting to self-destruct inside because she is constantly torn between the demands of being the "go-to" person who gets everything done at work, and the inner pull of her soul to be a wildlife photographer. She finally schedules a massage for herself, and then cancels it because her sister was having another relationship crisis.

If you said "yes" to any of the questions above, or if you can relate to Rebecca, you are overburdened with responsibilities. You've forgotten how to honor your own needs and if you do anything for yourself, you feel selfish. You're living the life that others expect of you. Your dreams have faded into a distant memory and you aren't even sure how to find meaning and direction.

Guilt floods in when you put even a small need of yours before those of your children, your friends, or your community. You agree to do even more for others to avoid hurting or disappointing someone, or ruffling the feathers of those who have depended on you.

You ignore your own potential and get uneasy when you think of stepping into your own power. After all, who do you think you are to be a famous wildlife photographer, best-selling author, or the most popular American travel guide in Italy?

You keep on keeping on with your obligations, but, little by little, resentment starts brewing with each request from your kids and your spouse. Oh no, now even more guilt piles up because how could you be resentful toward those you love? So you stuff those dreams once again.

You take care of your kids, and listen to your spouse about a difficult employee situation he has at work. You notice your back is hurting, and your head is pounding as you help your kids with their homework. Over time, the anger at your spouse begins to chip away at your marriage. The toll for silence or surrendering your power is indeed great.

The truth is that we teach people how to treat us. For years, you did everything to help your spouse. When the kids left their homework until the eleventh hour, you rushed in to help. When the church needed a substitute youth leader for the weekend, you said "yes."

Stop! If you don't take steps to ask for help, the stress will take a huge physical and emotional toll. You are basically robbing yourself of your own potential and the sad part is that you are failing to stand up for yourself.

"The greatest day in your life and mine is when we take total responsibility for our attitudes. That's the day we truly grow up." ~John Maxwell

Simplifying your life comes from drawing firm lines, with honesty, grace and respect, but drawing them nonetheless. You can expect conflict and resistance when you first change the rules with those who depend on you, but when you stand firm, the ones who love and care for you will come around.

Family Responsibilities

Ask yourself what obligations have you accepted...and why? Can someone else in the family begin to share some of these responsibilities? Maybe not entirely in the beginning, but perhaps they could help with part of the task.

Do you spend a lot of time ferrying kids from school to soccer practice and then to piano lessons? Is there an older child who has a driver's license that could help out? Your older daughter may not like to do this, but for your sanity tell her that you need her help. Then give that responsibility on certain days to your older child. (Do not give in to her grumbling. Stand firm.)

Another key point we often forget is that you are then teaching your older child that the world does not always revolve around her needs. Sometimes it is necessary to help others first. Teenagers need these lessons. So you are helping teach her about caring for her younger siblings while also encouraging and building her sense of responsibility. You may have to deal with teenage angst in the beginning, but if you hold fast to this request, the result is that everyone who is involved grows.

Be prepared for some ruffled feathers because you're changing the lay of the land and modifying expectations. The oldest may feel that you're trampling on her freedom, and the younger kids may be disappointed that mom isn't always there to pick them up. Recognize that when you want to make a difference in their lives, you must first make a difference in yours. You need to free up some time and energy for the more important things that you wouldn't miss for the world.

There are several side benefits when you stand up, simplify your schedule, and let go of the wheel:

- The younger children will eventually recognize that they can rely on another person besides mom,
- The teenager gains more confidence and feels needed,
- You get some extra time to start taking care of yourself by joining a book club, taking a nap, or going to a concert.

Friends and Community

The same goes for friends. You see your friends as understanding and supportive. However, if you have been the over-giver and now decide to draw some boundaries, expect some of them to push back with a little guilt trip, or by asking even more of you. Change is hard for anyone, no matter how much we love them, or they love us.

Look at this possible scenario. You agreed to have a sleepover this weekend for your friends' two kids, so she and her husband could finally have a date night. Due to a business associate's family emergency, you ended up taking his place on a last minute business trip. You are on the verge of coming down with a cold, and you are so glad to finally walk in your front door after a tough week.

You would really like having Saturday night to relax in bed and catch up on sleep, but you committed to the children's sleepover. If you don't take care of yourself, you know that cold is going to hit even harder. Instead of you taking care of someone else, you would like someone to take care of you, bring you some soup and find a good movie to watch on TV.

Just the thought of cooking, cleaning, providing entertainment, and getting everyone in bed at a reasonable hour is exhausting! So what do you do? Do you tell yourself that you made a promise, take a few Tylenol, and tough out the weekend?

No, you need to take care of yourself first. The best decision is to call your friends. Apologize and tell them that you need to cancel this weekend's sleepover. If they are good friends, you may want to explain a little, but do not over-explain or over-defend your position. No matter how you phrase it, doing so exposes your feelings of guilt.

Instead, stand strong, be honest, and don't give in. If you waffle, you send a mixed and confusing message that causes your friends to doubt the strength of your boundaries. Be firm, loving, and direct. You don't have to be on the defensive or tell every detail of why you need to opt out of the activities.

This is not easy to do if you've lived your life always being the responsible one. Also your friends may not know what to say because you have never said "no" before – ever! Just keep that conversation short and assure them that you'll reschedule when you're feeling better. By handling this situation kindly but firmly, you are standing up for what you need to do for yourself, and yet preserving a relationship and friendship that matters to you.

"If you take responsibility for yourself, you will develop a hunger to accomplish your dreams." ~Les Brown

OK, so you managed to handle that weekend situation. You got some rest and you are feeling better. Then more requests come in for your time and expertise. You pride yourself in being an active member of the community. You are afraid to turn down any request because you are known as being very cooperative and supportive.

A local charity asks you to draft a fund-raising proposal because they know you do this type of work professionally. You cannot handle any more projects and yet you do not know how to refuse.

It seems selfish not volunteer your skills when the charity needs help.

Supporting your community doesn't mean taking on all forms of responsibilities like a beast of burden. Instead, don't let the guilt of possibly disappointing someone guide your actions.

If you are doing this grudgingly, your resentment starts building. So it is best to remind yourself of your core values and priorities that you worked on in previous chapters. If there is not a match between the new request and your priorities, then graciously say, "No, thank you. I appreciate you thinking of me and I wish you the best of luck with that project."

Tell the truth with care and respect. It's important that you do not take on the responsibility of managing their reactions or their emotions. Most people find it hard to object when you wish them the best in their efforts, and they will more than likely move on to find someone else.

Client Responsibilities

Have you accepted work from a new client, but realize that this client's needs are not a good match for your services? Your intuition is flashing because even though you knew their work wasn't a good match, you were afraid to say "no"? After all, income is income, right?

Taking on more than you can handle means you are short-changing all your clients, old and new. When you spread yourself so thin, something has to give, and that will either be your health or the quality of your work. Either one is not an outcome that you would want.

Being afraid to turn down work always backfires. Taking on more work solely because you are afraid nothing else will come your way points to a fear of lack. You don't trust that the right client with the right work will be there when the time is right. So you accept any and every job that comes around. You doubt that the road will rise up to meet you, and you worry that the wind will not be at your back when you stand up for yourself by saying thank you, but "no."

Nothing is further from the truth. When you trust what you know is right, life has a way of bringing more good stuff your way. Opportunities filled with the potential for more abundance start flowing to you. You begin to attract better clients who respect your work and your boundaries. These will be the people who will pay you what you are worth and more. They value your expertise and those are the clients on which to build your reputation and business.

Setting Boundaries the Healthy Way

How can you start laying boundaries so you can do what's best for you? Here are few ideas:

1. When asked to take on yet another task, before answering, tell the person you need to review your schedule and you will get back to her tomorrow (or by next week). Then consider what this task will take to complete. Will this support your values and priorities, or take you in another direction? Giving yourself some breathing space allows you time to make the best decision for you.

2. State up front that you may not be able to help out. If you decide that going through with the request isn't in your best interests, it's best to say so at the time of asking. By giving them a heads-up that you're likely unavailable, it gives the people asking time to consider and develop other options.

3. Check in with your intuition. By giving yourself some space to think about the request, you have time to check in with what your inner wisdom is saying. Quiet your mind, see what you body is telling you and see how you are feeling. For many people, mornings are the strongest time to check in and discern the best decision. So before you go to bed, ask for the answer to this question. In the morning, check in to see if your

gut is telling you "yes" or "no." Trust your instinct. (The next chapter talks more about listening to your intuition.)

4. Measure the success of your setting boundaries experience by how you feel after you've turned down an invitation or request. Are you feeling reassured, relieved and comfortable with your decision? Are you glad you said "no"? Don't gauge your success by the reaction of the other person. You cannot control the emotions and feelings of another, only how you react and feel. Besides, thinking you can manage the feelings of another is shouldering yet another responsibility that isn't rightfully yours.

5. Ask yourself this question, "If I know the person won't feel rejected or hurt, would I refuse?" It's surprising how accurate our inner voice is when we make room for it to be heard.

6. Speak the truth firmly but respectfully. If you struggle with finding the right words to say, you may want to seek support from another friend to rehearse your answer. Again, don't over-explain but prepare yourself enough so that you come across with a firm but polite conviction.

7. Learn from your early successes with saying "no." If you've always been overly responsible or the family caregiver, this is new for you. Imagine a baby taking first steps. Be kind with yourself, but be observant. Most of the time, we feel conflict and uncertainty in refusing a request because we don't have the right words to refuse with truth and honesty. Once you lay down your boundaries a few times, review your progress. Check to see what kind of language works best and what tone of voice was most convincing. By getting a handle on the tools you need to take care of yourself, you will not be racked with conflict the next time you have to say "no." The old saying, "Practice makes perfect" still rings true.

Today's STRUT

(Simple Tips for your Remarkable Unique Transformation)

Becoming Aware of Your "Yeses"

1. This week become aware of every time you say "yes" when in fact you wish you would have said "no." Identify the smallest task and go back to the person and bow out of it -- graciously but firmly. Then you'll become even stronger and soon you'll be able to say "no" when you really do not want to do what's being asked of you.

2. Next time you are asked to do something you really don't feel you have time to do, tell the person you will get back with them by tomorrow. This will give you time to think. You will eventually get to the point of being able to be polite but firm when you know immediately that you do not want to or cannot take on any additional projects. For now, use the above techniques.

3. Say "yes" to something that you have wanted to do for yourself for a while. If you are not used to doing things for yourself, start small. Maybe you go out to the local coffee shop and treat yourself to a fancy coffee drink you love. Do one thing for yourself this week. Relax and enjoy the time.

Affirmations:

I have the courage to make choices that honor my needs, my desires, and my dreams.
I take responsibility for my own feelings. I'm responsible for my own life.
I do only what I can do, not what's expected of me.

Trusting Your Intuition and Guidance

Real-Life RUST
(Routines that Undermine Simple living Techniques)
- You feel that you have to do everything yourself. You can't trust anyone else to do it right.
- You need to figure out every possible scenario so you can make the right decision. You need to think about something logically and it's difficult to hear your intuition.

Simplify by:
- Being open to signs and symbols and learning to trust your intuition
- Slowing down to be able to hear guidance

"Your intuition will tell you where you need to go; it will connect you with people you should meet; it will guide you toward work that is meaningful for you – work that brings you joy, work that feels right for you." ~Shakti Gawain

Getting in Sync with the Universe

You are not alone. No recent story illustrates the universal connection between all living things than the extraordinary story surrounding the death of well-known author and conservationist, Lawrence Anthony.

Anthony was widely known as the "elephant whisperer" because of his unique ability to communicate with wild elephants, and his unending work to rehabilitate those injured and traumatized in the bush. He worked with rogue elephants, originally targeted to be shot because of their violent behavior. These creatures were rescued and given a new lease on life because of Anthony's love and patience.

When Anthony died in South Africa on March 2, 2012, two herds of wild elephants, who had not visited Anthony's house for 18 months, unfathomably trekked an estimated 12 hours through the Zulu bush to gather around his home on the Thula-Thula reserve. They stayed around in his compound for two days, standing together in what appeared to be a mourning vigil, and then dispersed.

"... perhaps the most important lesson I learned is that there are no walls between humans and the elephants except those that we put up ourselves, and that until we allow not only elephants, but all living creatures their place in the sun, we can never be whole ourselves." ~Lawrence Anthony, Elephant Whisperer

It was hardly a coincidence that these magnificent creatures would choose that particular time to travel to Anthony's house. They sensed the loss of a man that cared deeply for them, and traveled miles to say goodbye.

We live in an intelligent Universe. There are no "accidents." Instead synchronicities like the story above are signposts and markers reminding us that there's much more to life, living and the universe than we can sense with our five senses. Stories like these sound miraculous, but the truth is that when we get in sync with the Universe, every day is a working miracle.

The challenge is how to experience this. How do we still all the noise around us so we can be in tune with the wisdom and guidance, our intuition, and messages from God to experience all the miracles that happen?

It seems that everyone has an opinion. Some express them loudly, others keep theirs to themselves. Some insist that others come around to their way of thinking while others vociferously defend the right to hang on to their own opinions.

You have an opinion too, but if you are at all sensitive or empathetic, it may be harder to hear your own voice above all the others. For a sensitive person, surrounded by a barrage of conflicting opinions is like being caught in a windstorm, buffeted this way and that by gale and force winds, unable to catch your breath while you're being violently battered and bruised.

That makes it even more challenging to hear the most important but quietest voice of all -- the voice of your soul, the voice within. That voice never attempts to outshout or to be louder than the noises of fear, stress, and anxiety that rush in. The voice of your soul is like a gentle nudge, a thought that bubbles up softly from the unconscious -- that small, kind whisper that points you in a certain direction for your highest good.

Our intuition is our GPS on life's journey and when we wander off course, it speaks out to alert us that we're heading in the wrong direction. When we are on the right track, we feel that all is right with the world.

When we are on a less than ideal path, our intuition does whatever it can to get our attention. The voice of your soul doesn't yell because it believes in giving you freedom of choice. So how can you "hear" this inner voice? It takes practice to listen and learn how your spirit communicates with you. For me, I get a pit in my stomach when I've made a decision that's not in my best interest. For others, they may get tightness in their back, headaches, or maybe just a knowing that something is "off."

"You have to leave the city of your comfort and go into the wilderness of your intuition. What you'll discover will be wonderful. What you'll discover is yourself." ~Alan Alda

The lesson is to learn how to recognize these signs early on, so you don't need to experience major consequences. If you ignore the gentle voice for too long, you will probably get a wake-up call. At that point, the wake-up call could be an illness, a traumatic event, or a huge shock because by then that's the only way your soul can get your attention. When that happens, listen. Don't turn off the alarm because if you do, the consequences down the road could be very costly.

Jeannie was having financial problems. As a freelance graphic designer, her income fluctuated depending on the amount of work she had during the month. Having already maxed out her credit cards, she went into shock when she received a big bill for repairs to her six-year old car. It appeared that the only answer was for her to not have the car repairs done. She would need to temporarily take public transportation to work, even though that would add another hour to her daily commute.

A colleague offered to lend her $4,000 so she could get her car in working order. Jeannie did not know him very well, but he seemed to be a straight shooter. No repayment plan was discussed, only the subtle understanding that she was to repay it when she could. When she looked at the check he presented, alarm bells went off, and her inner voice said, "No, don't," but she went ahead and accepted the loan.

The car repairs were more than the initial estimate. Jeannie told her colleague about the additional cost and asked to borrow another $1,500. At this point, he was upset. He reluctantly agreed to the additional amount, but he immediately insisted on a repayment plan in monthly amounts exceeding what she could ideally afford.

Jeannie was in no position to bargain. After three months of making the payments on time she hit another bump in the road. She couldn't make the fourth payment. When she asked for a grace period, her colleague threatened to take her to court for failing to meet her obligations.

The colleague's original loan seemed like a simple solution to Jeannie's problems, but her inner guidance was saying "no." Her intuition was trying to get her to explore other options and not take what seemed like an easy solution. However, Jeannie ignored the message only to feel higher stress and have even more problems months down the road.

When Your Inner Voice Points the Way Forward

We've probably all had a time in our life when we did something like Jeannie, knowing a decision wasn't in our best interest. Have you ever had a feeling that you were meant for more? That life shouldn't be this hard? Or that we shouldn't have to take the stress or the abuse we're putting our bodies through?

Maybe you've outgrown your job and the responsibilities are crimping your creativity like old shoes that no longer fit. Or maybe you had buried your dreams of writing in order to raise your kids. Then you realize the kids have been out of the house for five years!

How do we access our inner voice, especially when we need guidance? How can we find ways to shine the light on the way forward, especially when everything seems foggy and unclear? The key is not to force an answer from within, but to open the channels of communication so that the gentle voice can be heard.

"Listen to your intuition. It will tell you everything you need to know." ~Anthony J. D'Angelo

Haley was offered a job that would take her out of her current career path and into a completely new field. She was comfortable and reasonably happy in her current job. The new job was exciting with lots of potential for promotion. Because the new job was with a start-up high-tech firm, Haley was worried about the company not being successful, or feared that her new position would be cut if the company ran low on funds. The deadline for giving an answer was approaching and she was struggling with what to do.

One day, as she was taking a walk, the questions kept churning in her mind. "Is this the right job for me? Will I be successful or happy? Should I accept the job?"

She passed by a magazine stand and saw the latest *Outdoors Magazine* which featured the latest snowboarding locations. A keen snowboarder, she picked up the issue and out fell a foldout ad with the following slogan, "Miracles Happen." She took that to be a green light to accept the new job and that decision changed her life beyond her wildest dreams.

Haley didn't have her answer immediately but she stayed open and she "knew" when she had received a sign about her job. Each person has different ways of connecting with their inner voice. Here are some suggestions to get in touch with what's best for you.

- Take a break from your routine and do something playful. You can play a game that engages a different part of your body or muscles. When we play, we open ourselves to improvisation and possibility and we allow different parts of our brain to take over.

- Go to sleep and pose the question you have to your subconscious. On waking, write down the dreams you may have had during the night, the symbols that appeared, or the messages you may have heard while sleeping. Do this first thing upon waking before the memory of your dreams fades away.

- Upon awaking in the morning, don't jump out of bed and run to your computer to check your emails. Instead, take a few minutes to check in with your thoughts and feelings. What messages are they giving you?

- Be open, pay attention to the signs. Do you keep seeing the same symbol? Does the same set of numbers keep turning up? Something that you were just thinking about occurs right in front of you. When that happens, acknowledge that your inner guidance is sending you a message. Pay attention to what is happening to see if you can get clearer on the message.

- If you don't have an immediate answer, don't panic. Instead, take a few deep breaths, get still and focus on your breathing for a few minutes. Phrase questions in such a way as to get positive and encouraging answers. Ask your intuition, "What is my next step for.....?" (You can add your specific situation to that question.)

- Carve time out within a day to have some quiet time to meditate or to just sit quietly and relax. Let go of the problem. If you do this regularly, in time you'll become intimately aware of the voice of your inner wisdom.

5.	Embrace the unknown. The right answer may take a completely different shape from what the rational and logical mind is expecting. By letting go of expectation and fully welcoming what comes forth, you'll be guided to solutions that may be clearer, easier to implement, and even more fun.

6.	If you're still torn between two answers, the message from within is the one that feels and sits right with your body and your heart. It's the one that leaves you calm and confident. The other answer may seem practical, but if it produces a slight dissonance, a sense of unease, a slight backache, or stiffness in the neck, your body is telling you that it is not the best solution.

7.   Practice listening to your inner guidance. Allow yourself to be guided for a full 24 hours by your intuition. For every decision you need to make or question you need answered, place your hand on your heart center and say quietly, "My intuition tells me to ....." Listen and when it feels right, follow the advice given to you by your inner guidance.

8.   For example, it's your day off and you may be asking if you should stay at home or join friends who are meeting for lunch. You're naturally shy and your tendency is to want to stay at home, but your intuition may say *"Have lunch out."* Follow through and you may find that you meet a friend's cousin at lunch. He is visiting from out of town and turns out to be exactly the person you have been hoping to meet. If you'd squashed that voice, you would have missed the gift.

9.   By doing practice runs like these, you're saying to the Universe, "Show me, I'm listening and I'm taking action." No matter how much doubt you feel, how torn and uncertain you are about the choices you have to make, give yourself permission to ask and stay open.

10.   The answer can take any form or shape. It may appear ridiculous at first but trust the message. Maintain a positive attitude, embrace the unexpected, and you will find yourself on a simpler, less stressful path sooner than you think.

Today's STRUT

(Simple Tips for your Remarkable Unique Transformation)

Learning to Trust Guidance from Within and Without

1. Record what you perceive as synchronistic events in a journal. Write down what you think is the message being offered. Next to it, write down any action that you take as a result of the guidance being offered. What were the results? Were they to your benefit?

2. What happened when you ignored those messages? Were the results positive or negative?
    11.
3. Determine the best way for you to hear your guidance. Practice with small questions and keep asking so when there is a big decision you know what to do to trust your intuition.

Affirmations:

I act without fail when divine guidance presents itself to me.
I clearly hear the messages sent to me from the voice within.
I am one with all life and all life is one with me.

The Power of Gratitude

Real-Life RUST
(Routines that Undermine Simple living Techniques)
- Your Boss/Client just gave your favorite project to someone else.
- You walk in the front door to find your friend swimming in your pool with your partner.

Simplify by:
- Becoming more aware of others and remembering to say "thank you" often.
- Taking a break. Take off your shoes. Think of something that makes you smile.
- Pausing in the evenings to talk to your plants, kids, and/or spouse. Tell them you appreciate them and offer them a hug.

"Cultivate the habit of being grateful for every good thing that comes to you, and to give thanks continuously. And because all things have contributed to your advancement, you should include all things in your gratitude." ~Ralph Waldo Emerson

Where awareness goes, energy flows. If you put more attention on your gratitude for others, you will not only appreciate yourself more, others will too. If you create the space for gratitude in your life by small gestures, you create an attraction--a boomerang effect, and it comes back to you.

What is the real lesson of gratitude? If you can truly appreciate others, you will begin to more fully appreciate yourself. **Gratitude is the one concept that can transform your life faster than anything else.** When you truly feel grateful, you feel blessed and full. The simple things in life are more meaningful. If you take only one thing from this book, it is to learn how to live in a place of gratitude – every day.

Get back to Basics

A simple way to bring gratitude into your life is to give thanks for the things you cannot live without.

If you could not breathe, all other worries and concerns would fade away pretty quickly. Take in a deep gratifying breath of air. Aren't you happy that you can breathe? Feel gratitude for air and breathing. Fill your lungs with fresh oxygen. Feel it filtering into your blood stream and being circulated in your body.

If there were no food to eat, our physical bodies would wither away. The rumble in your tummy would surpass any other worry you had. Take a moment and feel your body. Is it well-nourished and vibrant? A simple gesture of placing your hand over your stomach and being grateful for food, and your ability to digest, can bring your awareness to what is pleasant in life.

If clean water were scarce, you would spend most of your day looking for it just to stay alive. When you turn on the tap to refill your water bottle, be grateful for clean, abundant water. How does it taste? Swish it around in your mouth and appreciate its cool, wet and refreshing qualities.

Returning to the basics of survival can be a really simple way to bring gratitude back into your life. Since most of us currently live more complicated lives, take these same ideas and start being grateful for everything that is happening around you.

Be grateful when you find the item that you need is on sale; when you can finally walk again after badly spraining your ankle; or coming home to a silly pet that makes you smile after a hard day.

"No one particular religion has been able to secure the exclusive rights for the power of prayer. No matter who you are, we all have the ability to take advantage of this amazing

and wonderful power. Once you realize this, you will then be filled with the desire to help others realize this as well. More and more people are resonating with this understanding, and this could result in a more wonderful future for mankind. (165)" ~Masaru Emoto, The Secret Life of Water

Mr. Emoto's Water Experiment

Water is an interesting medium because it changes easily with an outside stimulus as simple as a swirl of a finger. Dr. Emoto took this several steps further by looking at water crystals before and after a verbal blessing. If you do a Google search for "Dr. Emoto Water Experiment" you can see what water does when it is thanked in several languages.

The entire premise of his study is applied to the human body because it is nearly 65%-90% water. If you continually embody a "thankful" existence, you literally change the makeup of the water in your body. Not only you, but others will benefit by hearing the two little words "thank you," too.

In one experiment, no words were spoken but instead "thank you" was taped to the bottle of water. The water crystals, after a few days, were transformed into a more elaborate crystalline form. Gratitude in the form of a written note works too! This gives us yet more ways to benefit from the power of living a grateful life.

When Bad Things Happen

Many times good things happen to good people. And, sometimes, bad things happen to good people. When you see your friend swimming with your partner, gratitude is usually not the first emotion you experience.

But if you practice gratitude regularly, you are more equipped to even out the ebbs and flows in your emotional reactions to situations. It's important to realize that while we have no control over some situations, we DO have control over our emotions to the situations.

Take Mr. Emoto's water example...how can you react to situations and bring positive vibrations to a difficult situation? Can you picture what is happening to the water in your body (all 90+% of it) as you yell at your cheating partner? It becomes a toxic environment. If you want to regain vibrant health and energy become aware of the power of your emotions. By walking away instead of yelling, you can avoid flooding your body with negative, toxic energy, and a lot of harmful stress.

This does not mean you should stuff your feelings. It is important to express your feelings but it is usually healthier and wiser to do so after cooling off. Who really suffers when you get emotionally unhinged? You do. The cheating partner has already made a decision to cheat. The boss or client has already made the decision to give your project away.

If you go ballistic, is that good for you? Some argue that it helps by getting angry, but remember how your body feels afterwards. The anger causes tight muscles, spiking of your blood pressure, and it's exhausting.

The better choice is to cool off and then address the situation and express your feelings. As soon as you can after an incident that brings up strong emotions, think of something that you are grateful for...even if it's just that you had real maple syrup on your waffles that morning.

 While learning to make behavior changes, keep in mind it takes a lot of practice to make perfect! When working on gratitude expect:

- To make mistakes!
- To face situations that challenge your ability to feel grateful.
- Miracles! Pat yourself on the back at every small improvement.

Gratitude at Work

Being grateful for our co-workers can be difficult at times. It's hard to appreciate people that give our favorite project to an associate, or someone that tells us what to do in a condescending manner. You may be underpaid, reprimanded, and unappreciated. Not to mention the very real potential of conflicting personalities. We choose our friends, but not our co-workers; unless of course you are the boss.

On a more positive note, many people do become friends with their co-workers over time. The majority of our waking hours are spent at work. Couldn't your work relationships become more rewarding if everyone practiced a little gratitude?

Here are a few suggestions for simple little tasks to bring gratitude to your work life. Chose those that are within your power to practice:

- A phone call to thank someone who helped you on a project
- Gracious welcome to a new client or someone you've been working with
- Thank your boss with a small piece of chocolate
- Bring surprise coffee to a meeting
- A token bonus in a paycheck for a job well done
- Send an "E-Card" to someone who has recommended you to a new client
- Send an email raving about a job well done and cc a manager or boss
- Stick a smiley face sticker on a co-worker's door

If you work in an office, one way to continually appreciate co-workers and employees is to set up an appreciation board. Employees can post notes and a "thank you" to staff. Some examples would be "Toni, thanks for always remembering everyone's birthday!" or "Jeremy, awesome job on the presentation last week!" These are posted in a public place for all employees to read.

Sometimes employees and co-workers want recognition for their contributions to a project or for their strengths. Get to know what is meaningful to them by asking them. They might be interested in having some control over what they are doing in their job. You could give top employees a new project within their area of interest. Or you could train someone for an Assistant Manager role. Depending upon the personality of the worker, this could be the best thanks they've ever received!

In the local news recently there was a great story about a man who had started his career with a restaurant at age 12, washing dishes and running errands. After 18 years with the business, he was saddened to learn it was closing. The owners were now elderly and had decided to sell the business.

The restaurant was only on the market a short time when the now 30 year old man decided he wanted to purchase it and run it as his own. The elderly couple took the restaurant off the market and decided to train their loyal employee as the new owner. How can you top that for gratitude? What an amazing story of loyalty, desire and gratitude!

Gratitude at Home

After a long day of neglecting ourselves, we can unknowingly bring negativity into our homes. Instead of bringing your work stress, clear your mind before coming in your front door.

Sing your favorite song at the top of your lungs. Go for a quick run before going home. Take a few minutes once you are home to wash up, change your clothes, and then interact with your loved ones. By taking a break to celebrate YOU, you bring a better perspective home with you each night.

Often times in relationships, arguments start because one person doesn't feel appreciated by the other. Remember it takes just a few moments to hug and listen to your loved ones. When cooking dinner, rub their back or ask if you can help. If they are busy, give them the space they need. Then check in later to see how they are doing. If you are grateful that they helped clean the house or pull the weeds in the back yard, don't keep it to yourself--tell them! We all want to feel appreciated and we seldom hear that enough.

We can get stuck in a rut of going to work, coming home, going to work, and coming home. Do something new and different—and not just on a Friday night. Bring home a little gratitude for your home or family -- a new board game, a slice of decadent chocolate cake, a new plant, or the latest movie everyone has been dying to see.

Make an announcement, "This is for being such a great (fill in the blank)...family, dog, house, or spouse!" Pets are so excited to see you at any time of the day. Take a moment to pet them and tell them you love them. A few minutes of attention goes a long way and actually makes us feel better. If you have time, walking in nature with your furry friend can clear the clutter from your occupied mind and change your perspective.

Dogs are perfect examples of the embodiment of love and devotion. If you really want to feel gratitude, visit a pet shelter. These animals are in danger of their lives, and they still get so excited to see a new person that stops to pet them, take them for a walk or offer a treat...maybe even adopt them! Once adopted, they are forever friends and show you gratitude every day. Is there anyone else can you think of that waits for you all day, is not upset with you for being gone so long, and is excited to see you no matter what your mood?

Gratitude for Nature and Earth

"When you arise in the morning, give thanks for the morning light, for your life and strength. Give thanks for your food and the joy of living." ~Chief Tecumseh

When was the last time you thanked the Earth for providing for your basic needs? Maybe some of these gratitude suggestions seem simple, but if we become more aware of all the things we take for granted, you will start to see miracles all around you.

It's fairly rare that people acknowledge where their food, clothing and shelter actually comes from. It is a very simple thing to add to your day.

Before eating, say a little blessing for your food. *"Mother Earth, I appreciate this meal. Thank you for providing for me."*

When walking outside for the first time each day. *"Mother Earth, I breathe your air into my lungs. Thank you for providing for me."*

When returning someone back to the Earth. *"Mother Earth, thank you for providing a body for this person. We return them to you."*

The simple act of standing outside and listening to the breeze, the birds, the insects and knowing everything has its place, **is** enough. We are all just visiting this blue planet, and when we think of this life and its impermanence, it's easy to be grateful for what we have.

Think about winter turning into spring, the delight of the first snow, the fullness of the rivers and streams with snow's melt, the humming bird at your feeder. We are always relieved by the changing seasons and in awe of nature's power. Sit with these feelings and give gratitude for your body and our senses that allow us to appreciate it.

Your relationship to nature is extremely basic. You need nature to thrive so you can thrive. So quickly a natural disaster can change lives, so give thanks for this perfect moment in time and nature's stability and will to survive at all costs.

Gratitude in Action

How can I begin to remember to be thankful when I'm just trying to get out of bed in the morning? Remember, start where you are. What is the simplest way to offer thanks? Start with the suggestions below. Work one of these into your life each day.

- Write on a mirror and say out loud, "Today, you are great!"
- Post notes in your lunch box "Are you smiling yet?"
- Put something special in your child's backpack with a note that says, "Thank you for being you."
- Text your spouse/mother/sister and tell them you love them.
- Every morning as your feet touch the floor say one thing you are grateful for.
- Before you fall asleep at night, think of something that happened that day for which you are grateful. There's always something no matter how tough your day was.

Every time you have negative thoughts, take that opportunity to be grateful. Remember, start where you are. Start transforming the sticky black negative statements into gold by remembering to say something you are grateful for in place of the negativity. They say that we only forget to remember again, so don't beat yourself up. Just start remembering again.

The changes we start to see in our behaviors and our energy level when we begin to offer gratitude are monumental. In fact, we may start to see others reciprocating and offering gratitude freely to others.

"Be thankful for what you have; you'll end up having more. If you concentrate on what you don't have, you will never, ever have enough." ~ Oprah Winfrey

Recognizing and Accepting Gratitude

How many times has someone tried to thank you and you respond with a wave of your hand saying, "It's nothing." It is NOT 'nothing!' In order to show gratitude to others it's necessary to accept it, too. Otherwise you're not completing the circle.

If you are waving off thanks, ask yourself why. Is it because you didn't mean to help the other person? Not likely! Is it because you can't accept appreciation for your work? Remember the first sentence of this chapter:

What is the real lesson of gratitude? If you can truly appreciate others, you will begin to more fully appreciate yourself.

If you cannot accept gratitude, you are not fully appreciating others, and you are not appreciating yourself and your contributions. Maybe you grew up thinking it was vain to truly accept a compliment. (It's not...it's healthy.) Start looking for moments of appreciation in your life; both internally and externally. Start building upon those moments until they become *important*.

When someone blows off your gratitude, emphasize that you really do appreciate their efforts and appreciate them. Once we stop the cycle of not accepting, we start connecting better with ourselves and with others.

Feeling truly grateful allows us to appreciate everything from the basics to our daily miracles. Gratitude, more than anything else, will allow you to be able to live simply. Focus on gratitude every day until it becomes a regular part of your thoughts. There is tremendous power in gratitude. Live it and share it.

Today's STRUT *(Simple Tips for your Remarkable Unique Transformation)*

What are you grateful for?

Start a gratitude journal. Every night before you go to sleep, list five things for which you are grateful. Do this every night (and look for new things to add to your list). These do not have to be major things. You can be grateful for finding a parking space in a crowded lot. You can be grateful for finding the solution to a work problem ten minutes before your boss asked!

Write out a few gratitude statements and post them on your bathroom mirror.

- I am grateful for my health.
- I am grateful that my friend.
- I am grateful that I can learn how to de-stress.

Remind yourself of your two or three chosen statements and write them on a post-it or put an alarm reminder in your phone to repeat your gratitude phrases. Take a few minutes during the day to take off your shoes, close your eyes, and focus on your breath. Repeat your statements until your mood starts to change.

Post one nice thing about a co-worker in the lunch room, or send an e-card to a colleague during a break. Create a feeling of gratitude and soak up the feelings.

Get outside and breathe fresh air! Thank Mother Earth for supporting you.

If you are not feeling better yet, go back to the beginning of this chapter...rinse and repeat, repeat, repeat!

Affirmations:

I am grateful to be alive today.
I recognize simple pleasures in my life and give thanks for them.
My relationships with others improve as I recognize and thank others.
I accept gratitude from others whole-heartedly.
I appreciate me!

86,400 Seconds a Day

Real-Life RUST
(Routines that Undermine Simple living Techniques)
- You work so hard, but have never have time to relax.
- You always have so many things to do. Your marriage is suffering because you are always working.

Simplify by:
- Becoming aware of your breathing.
- Completing one small task that you have been putting off.
- Being grateful for little and big things in your life.

"What comes first, the compass or the clock? Before one can truly manage time (the clock), it is important to know where you are going, what your priorities and goals are, in which direction you are headed (the compass). Where you are headed is more important than how fast you are going. Rather than always focusing on what's urgent, learn to focus on what is really important." ~Author Unknown

"There's not enough time in a day."
"Time flies."
"I'm never on time, there's just so much to do."
"I'm running just to stand still."
"I have no time to breathe."
"How am I going to live my purpose when I'm so busy doing everything else for everyone else?"
"Who am I?"

Are these phrases familiar? How often do you say things like this to yourself each day, either consciously or subconsciously? What patterns are you setting into motion by repeating these phrases and drumming them into your subconscious?

Each of us has exactly 86,400 seconds in a day. How you spend those seconds (that add up to days which add up to months which add up to years) determines if you move toward your dream life or stay stuck in the RUST.

Here's a fun exercise. The ancient Egyptians believed that the soul was judged by Ma'at, Goddess of Truth, Balance and Order. The heart of the deceased, representing one's conscience, would be weighed against a single, ostrich feather, to see if the soul was worthy to move on to the afterlife, or if it would be devoured by a demon, if found wanting.

Borrowing this metaphor, visualize gathering all your thoughts and spoken statements about not having enough time, and bundle them onto a scale. Now bundle all your positive thoughts and words about having more than enough time and imagine those on the other side of the scale. Which would tip the balance?

For most of us, it's a safe bet that we think or talk more about lack and not having enough time. There's no demon waiting to swallow us for this imbalance, but it is very important to realize how much energy we put into the negative. Every moment in life is unique, like snowflakes, and no moment is like the one that comes before or the one that follows.

Whether you are shuttling your kids to their soccer games, managing a second home in the country, or overseeing 20 employees at work, our normal mode of operation is to react to what happens during the day instead of living by design.

This doesn't mean that you turn your back on your responsibilities, and run away and hide. Neither does it mean you fill your Kindle with time management books and courses. What's important is that you start becoming aware of what's happening. If you are stressed and never seem to have enough time, you are probably out of alignment with your priorities.

Simplifying your time is about getting your life to a place where it runs smoothly. You decide what activities you do because they fit with the type of life you want. This is about putting your energy into choices that enhance your life and those of the ones you love.

Now you might be saying, "I do not have a choice. The mortgage has to get paid. My son starts college in a few months. I would love to quit my job and start my own business, but I live in the real world!"

Yes, it is true that we aren't able to magically transport ourselves to a perfect world, with wonderful careers, understanding kids, and all the time to live our dreams. We all live in a real world with real demands. However, if we don't take responsibility for how we spend our time, it slips away, and that dream of having your own business or traveling the world will never happen. So it's not about doing and having everything instantly. It's about making better choices, one at a time.

Do you need to enroll your kids in soccer, ballet, swimming, and violin lessons all in the same month? Together decide which they enjoy and which you feel would help them the most this month. Choose only a couple activities for them. They can focus on additional activities later.

This allows you some time to enjoy a yoga class, lunch with a friend, or time to read the book you bought three months ago. Nurturing yourself renews your love of life and makes you a more exciting spouse, mother, sister and daughter. It's not being selfish. It's taking care of yourself, so you can fully give to those you love.

There are also some of you out there that overfill your dance-card. In addition to working long hours, you have weekend workshops, lunches, dates, PTA meetings, support groups, and networking meetings. Whew! Be honest now...did you even have any time to assimilate what you learned in that weekend workshop once it was over?

If you are serious about simplifying your time, commit to having more space for the things that matter and the time to be with the ones you love most. Some of the most precious moments in life are to be found by relishing and appreciating where you are right here and right now.

"Until you value yourself, you won't value your time. Until you value your time, you will not do anything with it." ~M. Scott Peck

When you are stacking the shopping cart with groceries for the family, feel appreciative that you are able to make healthy food choices while you're shopping. Taking time to feel grateful is one of those major internal shifts and it creates a powerful energy to propel you toward a simpler, happier life.

Breathe...consciously

Are you aware that there is a space, like a pause between notes on a music sheet, between each breath in and each breath out? It's in that space that there's no conflict and where all potential rests.

Try this. No matter what you're thinking right now, stop reading and take a deep breath in and then release that breath. Now take another deep breath in and hold it for a count of five. Then slowly breathe out.

Those of you who love music know that the pause is just as important as all of the notes, because that moment, when the world-class pianist raises his hand, gives us a brief time to reflect and fully savor the music.

In that universe of space between breaths there is choice. You can choose to let the runaway train of your fears and anxieties dictate your next moves. Or you can tap into your unlimited potential and pick a new, positive, supportive thought that sparks a new direction of actions.

Conscious breathing is powerful. In *The Miracle of Mindfulness: An Introduction to the Practice of Medication*, renowned Zen master, poet, author, peace and human rights activist, Thich Nhat Hanh writes, "Your breathing should flow gracefully, like a river, like a water snake crossing the water, and not like a chain of rugged mountains or the gallop of a horse. To master our breath is to be in control of our bodies and minds. Each time we find ourselves dispersed and find it difficult to gain control of ourselves by different means, the method of watching the breath should always be used."

Do whatever it takes to schedule five minutes into your day to just sit and be. Focus on your breath and relax. The physical, mental, and spiritual benefits of this are immeasurable.

Celebrate When You Say "No"

Celebrity author, motivational speaker and spiritual teacher, Wayne Dyer, is constantly besieged with requests from everything from donating to a good cause, attending a gathering or party, reading manuscripts submitted by unknown authors, to praying by the bedside of a dying patient.

All of these are good causes, but instead of being constantly on the go, Dyer makes wise choices. He declines the request if he feels he cannot be fully present at a particular event. When he does decide to participate, he relishes every moment, from the ride over, his time at the event, mingling and speaking with people, and thoroughly enjoying everything from start to finish.

How many times have you done something you wished you had said "no" to? Have you attended a gathering you really wanted to avoid, and ended up being sulky and miserable because you really wanted to be somewhere else? Be willing to say "no" without feeling you need to explain your decision.

Realize that if you can't say "no," your "yes" doesn't amount to much. When you say "no," be gracious, be firm. If later you happen to change your mind about that situation, the people who invited you in the first place will more than likely eagerly welcome you again.

Karen needed more space. She had adopted two cats, and felt that she was earning enough to afford a bigger apartment. There was a bigger apartment available in her building. She was in the middle of a very important project, and felt that it would not be wise to add the major task of packing and moving right now. She politely passed on that apartment. Later she felt she made a mistake in not taking that apartment.

The solution was quite simple. Rather than fretting over her earlier decision, all she did was inform her landlord that she was now ready. Karen asked to be put on the waiting list for a bigger space. She also told her friends and colleagues about her intention. By trusting that something would come along, she ended up attracting an even better space than she would have had with that first apartment.

Stop Procrastination

Have you reached into your closet, with only 20 minutes left to be out the door, to find that the pair of pants you plan to wear is missing a button at the waistband? You forgot to sew the button on over the weekend. Ugh!

Or you're rushing out of the door for an important presentation. You planned on reviewing your notes on your morning commute and you discover that you forgot to charge your iPad. AAHH!

Or you're missing that pivotal piece of paper that had the scribbled cell number of an important prospect you finally met after weeks of planning. You are frustrated that you didn't take one minute and add the prospect to your phone contacts.

Your tax return is due in four days and you are starting to feel a panic attack coming on because you did not get your documents together sooner. Your tax preparer is busy with clients who made their appointments months ago. Yes, you can probably file an extension but you also may face a penalty because of the delay.

"Procrastination is one of those excuses, born of fear, that we use to keep ourselves stuck." ~Wayne Dyer

These little mishaps always seem to happen at the most crucial moments. They throw you off your game, dropping you into a blue funk and robbing you of the energy you need.

Procrastination is so common. It seems easy to ignore that little task because you are "just too busy right now." Other bigger tasks loom over you and take priority.

Maybe at the time you thought, "It can wait, it's just not that important," which may be true at the time, but later those little tasks have a way of screaming to demand your attention.

When you finally get down to completing the task you have been avoiding, you discover that:

- Completing it didn't take as much time as you thought it would
- It wasn't as difficult as you had imagined in your head
- You felt a great weight lift off your shoulder
- You wasted emotional and mental energy worrying about it and then beating yourself up about not getting it done.

You've been carrying all that baggage unnecessarily because of avoiding a little task or many little tasks. What unfinished tasks are nagging at you? You can reduce your stress level and simplify your day by:

- Clearing the mess on your desk
- Starting your blog for which you've already chosen a witty title and name
- Donating the old clothes that are a deadweight in your closet
- Making the phone call you have been avoiding
- Taking down old posters and hanging new, inspirational ones

- Backing up the files and folders on your computer in the cloud, or on an external hard drive. (If this one is on your list, do it NOW. Replacing lost or damaged computer files is extremely stressful, time consuming, and frustrating. Some files can never be replaced, so do this today.)

Once you face these little annoyances, it is surprising how much freer you feel and how much more time you have. Commit to getting your most nagging task done today. Then move on to the next one.

Mark the task on your calendar, or hire a personal organizer or virtual assistant to do it for you. Just decide how it's going to get done and then do it. As Nike's famous slogan says, "Just Do It!" and then you can give yourself a high-five afterwards.

Simplifying is Easier with Schedules

Do you love to live spontaneously? You may thrive on last minute deadlines, chaos and feel that you are at your best when under pressure. Routine sounds like a bad word in your vocabulary, and as you've read in this book, some repeated old behaviors can keep you from reaching your goal to simplify.

Yet you are finding that while spontaneity and improvising are fun and challenging, you also see that you need to spend precious time putting out fires regularly from unanticipated problems. They are not serious issues but each time it happens it seems to take more of your energy to blanket these fires and you are getting suffocated by the smoke!

How does a free spirit shift into a schedule? The key is to start small. Don't expect to have a healthy, working routine for every aspect of your day. Start with the one that you can manage most easily, i.e., establish a ritual for getting to bed by a certain time.

Make the experience of sticking to this new routine a comfortable and enjoyable one, by preparing hot chocolate to sip in bed, settling in with relaxing music or a good book, and make your bed extra comfy so you'll slip into it with pleasure and gratitude. Stick with this routine for at least three to four weeks before adding anything new. You'll find by doing one activity for 21 days, it starts to become a habit.

Once you realize that having some routine in your day can and will produce many benefits, you'll be encouraged to stick with this. Look at which areas are causing the most stress and tackle those first.

ABC Priorities

If getting out the door in the morning is challenging, take 10 minutes the night before and identify what needs to get done the next day. Every night before you go to bed, list out everything you need to do the next day, both for work and for personal tasks. Then group them into these three categories:

A - Absolutely must be done tomorrow (not necessarily what you'd like to get done). These tasks mean that if your day is winding down and these are not yet finished, you need to put on a pot of coffee and stay up all night to complete. Your "A" priorities are that important.

B - Tasks you would like to get done tomorrow, but are not absolute musts.

C - Other tasks. These tasks could and should be delegated to others if at all possible. (Remember you're empowering those people too when you delegate.)

Keep this list with you during the day, so you can look at it often. If a request or a new assignment comes up during the day, and you agree to do that task, identify it as an A, B, or C, write it on your list, and take action.

Work on your "A" priorities first, and then move on to your "B" priorities if there is time. Cross off items as soon as you have them finished.

With these simple steps, you're impressing on your conscious and your subconscious what needs attending to and in what order. That way, during the day, you can move smoothly from one priority to another. It's not uncommon that once you've identified your tasks before you go to sleep, solutions to pressing problems start to bubble up. When you wake up you have answers and you are ready for your day.

Make sure your phone is charged, you have your briefcase ready, and the files you were working on are in your briefcase. Set the coffee maker to auto-brew, and know what you will wear tomorrow. These are all little things, but they add up. If these are taken care of the night before, the next morning is so much easier.

There are so many ways to simplify your work. Some call for doing less to create more time for yourself, others call for breaking "established" rules and making your own.

Today's STRUT
(Simple Tips for your Remarkable Unique Transformation)

Prioritize to Eliminate Procrastination

Pay attention to how you spend your time. Take any week in your calendar and block off every necessary or meaningful activity, i.e., work, meditation time, business meetings, church, Friday night family time, Saturday date night, etc. Then look at everything else.

Circle any activities that you can do without. How many hours do those extra activities take up? You can use that extra time to dust off and complete a project or task you've been avoiding.

Begin working with the ABC Priority system so you know what needs to get done and when.

Spend a few minutes thinking about how you can reallocate your time. Complete the following sentences:

I use my time unwisely when I...

I want more time to.....

I can free up one hour per day/week if I (write in something that would feel fairly easy to give up to get started. Hint: Give up an hour of TV a day and you'll be amazed at how much extra you can get done.)

Affirmations:

My time is one of my most precious assets and I use it wisely, positively and productively.
I have all the time I need to accomplish everything I need to do today. I have time left over to relax and appreciate my life and my loved ones.
I create space and time for more creativity, meaning, and expansion in the important areas of my life.

Working 8 to Late

Real-Life RUST
(Routines that Undermine Simple living Techniques)
- You've lost your passion for your work. You feel empty and have lost touch with your dreams.
- You are overly responsible. You don't know how to delegate or ask for help.

Simplify by:
- Pursuing work that is meaningful to you. Evaluate what changes you can make to do work you love.
- Prioritizing your work and delegating as much as possible to others.
- Communicating your needs with family and with business associates and co-workers.

"In addition to balancing work and family, women need to think about their own health and their own well-being." ~Dana Hurst

Your boss walks into your office and says, "Sara, I need a detailed report for sales on Product X by 1:00 today so I can review before my meeting with our newest customer." It's 9:00 a.m. and this is easily a six-hour job. Then a co-worker asks for your advice on how to handle an extremely angry employee. Your weekly report is normally due by noon and it's obvious you are not going to be able to handle all the requests flying at you.

Overwhelm...whether you're juggling the requests of three other managers, or taking last minute requests from your customers to keep them happy, it can be easy to hit overwhelm.

If you are an entrepreneur, the lines blur between the necessary day-to-day routine tasks, and mapping out your vision and business strategy. You find yourself running just to stand still -- not moving backwards, but not moving ahead either.

For those of you climbing the corporate ladder, you may find yourself weighing how much you've given up over the years to arrive at where you are today. You spent years working endless hours and traveling for business trips, while your kids somehow grew up in the blink of an eye.

Regardless of where you are in your career or business path, we share common fears, worries and frustrations. We live in a chaotic, demanding world where exhaustion is the new normal. Gratification has to be nano-second fast or you find yourself trailing behind a competitor's latest and greatest accomplishment. We are overwhelmed and know that something is lacking – we just don't know what it is.

If you come home at the end of the day in tears and unhappy, or irritated over the slightest comment from your spouse, something clearly isn't right. Maybe you feel your life is passing you by. You hear about your friends going out to the latest concert and, here you are, pouring another cup of coffee to be able to finish the reports that were due at noon earlier today.

Even if you can keep up with the high-speed work treadmill, you are completely exhausted by Friday night and all you want to do on the weekend is to sleep or zone out in front of the television. This is not the life you had imagined.

If you are not doing work you love – whether as an employee or as a business owner, overwhelm and stress seem to multiply by the hour! You want to fly in the face of boredom and routine and take flight, but you don't even know where to start.

How could you possibly do what you love when you have the car payment, the mortgage, and your student loan payments that are due every month? You are good at several different things but you are so stressed you are not sure which to pursue...so you stay stuck in your routine.

If you are one of the lucky ones who are totally passionate about what you do, you are miles ahead of many. However, you may still find that passion alone doesn't power the boat or keep the business afloat. It still requires budgeting, accounting, delegating, finding the right help, negotiating leases, reviewing projections, schmoozing with your banker, anticipating trends, and figuring out your clients' needs. You wonder where the fun went in your business, as you slowly get sucked into the quicksand of routine.

"Your work is to discover your work and then with all your heart to give yourself to it." ~Buddha

No matter which scenario is yours, at some point we all feel the pain of loneliness, lack of time, work-life imbalance, stress from work overflowing into our personal time (and vice-versa), fear of failure, fear of success, or all of the above! This can easily become a complex quilt and, for many, the threads are coming undone and the edges are fraying.

How in the world do you begin to simplify your life when it's this complicated? How do you invite an ease and flow into your work, and work the ease back into your personal time?

Creating Value in Your Life

Hold this thought. Your work isn't about what you have to do. It should fully and wholly be about who you are and what you are here to share with the world. At its best, it should be a reflection of you and your talents and skills.

Your work should be about creating value, not just for your clients, but also for your own life. As you go through your day at work, use this as the filter or a litmus test for every decision – big or small – that you make. Ask yourself, "Will this add value to my life?" and also "Am I being of service in some way?"

Granted, when you first start this exercise, you may see a lot of incongruences. In the beginning you may still have to do the job, project, or task at hand. But be aware of how much time you spend doing something that you don't really feel is valuable to you. If you answer those two questions with anything less than a positive response, perhaps it's time to re-evaluate.

If you're looking to escape a humdrum job or one with stress overkill, you may be tempted to cut all ties in one fell swoop. Unless you have substantial savings or you are crystal-clear about what you want to do next, taking baby steps may be the simpler and wiser solution.

Jenna owns a very successful consulting business. She was the go-to person for a large number of clients with whom she had built solid relationships over the years. They knew they could always rely on her for expert service and advice. Jenna was very responsive and met the requests of her clients – usually whenever they called.

After doing this work for 20 years, she longed for a change. She had always loved writing. She dreamed of walking away from her business, buying a cottage in the woods, or moving to an island to write by the ocean.

A retreat into the woods hinted of a simpler life, but Jenna is a real extrovert and relishes the company of people. Chopping wood, carrying water, and playing a reclusive author-in-the-making would create no long-lasting joy in her life.

Instead, she whittled down her client list and focused on a handful of her long-term clients. With the extra time, she joined a writer's group in her local community where she met fellow writers with whom she enjoyed brainstorming and exchanging ideas.

She was inspired to write short stories. She received constructive criticism from her writers' group and entered writing competitions. Her stress level dropped. She was having fun again. The joy she felt from her writing brimmed over into her consulting business. She regained her zest for meeting her clients' needs and provided them with fresh, creative, and unique ideas.

Was value created? Absolutely! Jenna was still earning money. Her clients appreciated her renewed zeal. She found a new group of like-minded friends, and most importantly, she was having fun sharpening her writing skills and finding her muse.

Creating value in your work doesn't mean solely focusing on making more money. Value means doing what is necessary to take care of you. It could mean taking more time for you, making changes so you have less stress in your day, asking for more support, or having more fun. It is about taking small steps so you take better care of you.

Get Paid to Be You

Does your work resonate with you (whether you work for yourself or for someone else)?

Or do you put on your game face at work just to get through the day?

Do you look forward to another day at work with a bounce in your step?

Or have you changed so much that work now feels as uncomfortable as a pair of old jeans you've outgrown?

Are you able to truly express your gifts and talents through your work?

If your work doesn't tap into the uniqueness that is you, you're going to be bored, unhappy or frustrated -- not exactly a recipe for success.

Identify the unique talent that you can provide as a service. Maybe you're good with animals or with seniors. Perhaps numbers come easily for you, or you can sit down and draw a fabulous illustration in minutes. Whatever it is, you have a unique talent that the world needs.

Work becomes so much simpler and so much more fun when you tap into that talent. When you're proud of being who you are and what you are, you will attract the kind of clients who will resonate with you.

Warning: Do not succumb to thinking that you could not possibly make a drastic change in your life. Are you happy right now? Are you satisfied living your life exactly as it is today? (Probably not or you wouldn't be reading this book.)

Just let the ideas begin to percolate. If you need help in making a major work shift, visit http://DonnaJDavis.com for my Creative Self-Employment coaching sessions.

Empower Yourself and Others by Delegating

If you are an entrepreneur, you wear a lot of different hats. You're the marketing specialist, the public face of your business, the buyer, the bookkeeper, and the inventory manager. If you continue doing everything yourself, you'll be stretched so thin, you will end up a shadow rather than a presence in the marketplace.

There are many distractions in our work life. There are always "little tasks" that need doing. Completing them promotes a sense of accomplishment. Yet at the end of the day or at the end of the week, you may find that you haven't really moved forward in building your business. You were focused on secondary priorities instead of those that will build a client base and increase sales.

"Set priorities for your goals. A major part of successful living lies in the ability to put first things first. Indeed, the reason most major goals are not achieved is that we spend our time doing second things first." ~Author Unknown

Take a deliberate step back and ask yourself, "What are my core strengths?" If you're good with design but hate balancing the books, delegate the bookkeeping. With virtual assistants and help available online, there are few excuses for not hiring the extra help you need.

You have access to skilled freelancers around the world at highly competitive rates. By planning well you can work with someone halfway around the world who is 12 hours ahead of you. When you start your morning, the tasks you needed done can be ready and completed. You can stay in contact via email or Skype, have real-time conversations, and share files – the possibilities are endless.

Delegating work is not self-indulgent. It's actually simplifying your work by putting a support system in place to take over the jobs that are not aligned with your core strengths or your priorities. You may find it hard to release control or ask for help. You may feel you have to do almost everything yourself. Realize, however, that you are empowering yourself by freeing up your energy to concentrate on your strengths while empowering others so they can offer their skills and earn some income.

It is harder to delegate work if you are a paid employee, unless you are a manager or high up on the rungs of the corporate ladder. In such a situation, how do you engage your core strengths to be more effective or build a support system if assigning work to someone else is not an option?

First, understand that it is a myth that working long hours at frenetic speeds is productive. The fact is that overwork produces declining returns. Recognize that one of your core strengths is your energy and creativity, and you support those strengths by building in time to refresh and relax at work.

Here are some simple steps. Instead of eating at your desk, make the time to take lunch daily and engage in an activity not linked to work. You could take a walk in a park, listen to relaxing music, read a book, sketch or write in a journal, eat with a friend. Give yourself a mental break.

Ensure you have healthy snacks at your desk so you don't give in to the temptation of the vending machines. Always, always, have a bottle of water. If you are stressed, drinking a large glass of refreshing, cold water makes a huge difference in how you feel.

Set aside blocks of time for you to fully focus on your job responsibilities. Kindly but firmly tell friends and family that you are not available during set times (unless there is an emergency). This will help you eliminate non-essential interruptions.

With greater focus and attention, you will soon find that you are accomplishing more by the end of the day. The added benefit is that you will have energy left over for the evening.

Stop the Work-Life Bleed

Set your boundaries. This is especially difficult for those who work from home (something that more and more of us are doing now).

If you have a separate room for your home office, you may be able to close the door, but if you are not observing your work and personal boundaries, you still are not 100% present for your family. Plus there is always the temptation to head back in the office to finish that one last invoice.

Those who work in an office are just as susceptible to the work-life bleed. Even if you say goodnight to your colleagues, turn off the lights, and head home, if you carry the burdens of your work home, either in your briefcase or in your head, you aren't leaving work at work.

How do you make the break? How do you stop work from bleeding into your personal life?

By stepping into an environment that is diametrically and completely different from your work environment, you fully convince your mind and your body that you've left work.

Don't underestimate how much the look and feel of things around you impacts your inner balance. If you have a spare room, you can create a little sanctuary for yourself to enhance relaxation and to feed your soul. This can be a little room in which you install a small water fountain, a tabletop rock garden, or sweet smelling flowers.

It could be an indoor herbal garden filled with little pots of useful kitchen herbs. Or it could be a serene space for meditation with a simple, inexpensive mat and a meditation pillow.

It may be setting up an easel and working off the stress of the day by letting your inner artist loose. It could be a comfy chair outdoors where you can sit and sip a cup of tea and listen to the birds or feel the gentle breezes.

If space is limited, create a little privacy by using curtains and fabric as a room divider. Alternatively, how about creating a simple altar on a small side table?
Add something unique and fun every week or move things around occasionally. Change the theme of your altar once a month. The key is to create a visual treat for your eyes and a space to honor the soul. Simple, easy changes.

Building Support through No-Stress Networking

We've all heard how important networking is and the all familiar "meet and greet." Even if you know all the benefits of networking, do you get a pit in your stomach at the thought of having to put on your happy face and mingle with a group of strangers with whom you may have nothing in common? If the thought of working a room makes you break out in hives, you're not alone.

If you're naturally shy, you fall into the 20% of the population born with a tendency towards shyness. However, it's drummed into you that, love it or hate it, building key business relationships through networking is crucial to building or sustaining a business or improving career prospects.

How can you shift this into something you can enjoy?

- Think outside the box
- Make your own rules
- Create groups that you're comfortable with
- Borrow a leaf from Meetup.com

Meetup.com has revolutionized the way people get together. It matches people with shared interests, offers easy tools, plans meetings and forms clubs in local communities or anywhere around the world.

These groups can be for people interested in hiking, cultivating urban gardens, voluntary beach cleaning, or meeting to discuss shared business interests. In settings like these, it's easy to get over the initial awkwardness that you might encounter when meeting a total stranger in the more traditional events.

How about starting your own Meetup group in your local area? If you are a personal organizer new to the community you can set up a Meetup group "De-clutter by Design" to share easy ways to remove clutter, offer ideas featuring cool and hip accessories for organizing, share your Pinterest boards, discuss using all-natural products to spring clean, and so on.

This is "no-stress networking." You are already on familiar ground with the participants. It's a subject in which you enjoy talking about, you can easily establish yourself as an expert, and you are reaching out to your community by offering a service.

Today's STRUT
(Simple Tips for your Remarkable Unique Transformation)

Working Smarter

1. Write down three ideas that you can make to simplify your life at work during this next week. Examples are hiring a virtual assistant, planning out work the night before, delegating one task, asking for help, or organizing your desk.

2. Pick the easiest step and implement it tomorrow. Once that is in place, put the next one into practice. At the end of the week, see how you feel. See what worked and what didn't. The goal is to de-stress in little ways throughout your day.

3. If you are not doing work that you love, acknowledge that. Begin exploring ways that you can bring what you love to do back into your life. Maybe you do this as a hobby. Maybe it's time to start that business you have been dreaming of.

Affirmations:

My work is aligned with what I value most in life.
I have the courage to love what I do and do what I love.
I easily find the support I need to make my work simpler and more enjoyable.

Money and A-bun-dance!

Real-Life RUST
(Routines that Undermine Simple living Techniques)
- You work hard. You see something you like and buy it. You'll deal with credit card bill later.
- You have no idea how much money you really spend each month.
- You don't feel you deserve abundance because.....(fill in the blank)

Simplify by:
- Becoming aware of your spending habits
- Only buy what you really need and make sure they are meaningful to you

"Prosperity depends more on wanting what you have than having what you want." ~Geoffrey F. Abert

When you hear the word "money" what's your first reaction? Do you feel a pit in your stomach because you seem to have an ongoing struggle with money, bills, and debt? Or are you hopeful and excited because with money you can help so many others, and do so many good things in your community?

Identify Your Beliefs About Money

Those two reactions span the gamut of feelings surrounding "money." Unless you've done a money or prosperity exercise before, most people are not even aware of some of the underlying ways our thoughts about money control our outer actions.

Do you subconsciously believe money is "the root of evil"?
Are you afraid that friends and family members will change their opinion of you when you are successful and making a lot of money?

Are you concerned that you will lose your values if you make a lot of money?
Do you feel you deserve having money -- a lot of it?
Or do you feel money is for others, just not for you?

You are Worthy

Probably one of the most destructive thought patterns that prevent us from living a simple life is feeling that we don't deserve abundance. Yes, this book is on how to simplify our lives, so I'm not defining abundance as having four houses, two fancy cars, and every new electronic device imaginable.

Abundance means different things to different people. My definition of true abundance is being grateful for all my blessings, creating a life I love, and having the time and energy to enjoy those people and things that are important to me. It is about having great health, vibrant energy, low stress, love, and laughter.

When we struggle to pay even our basic bills, something is wrong. Maybe it was our religious upbringing. Maybe we did some things earlier in our life that we regret or caused financial strain. Maybe it's because we don't feel there is enough to go around. Regardless of where the belief that you are not worthy of abundance came from, it's time to let that go. The Universe wants to shower us with unlimited blessings. We block it for many reasons.

The topic of feeling worthy to receive is beyond the scope of this book. Many books have been my guide through my prosperity journey. My favorite is *"The Four Spiritual Laws of Prosperity: A Simple Guide to Unlimited Abundance,"* by Edwene Gaines. Another book that taught me universal principles is *"The Dynamic Laws of Prosperity,"* by Catherine Ponder.

There are many current books and DVDs on the Law of Attraction. Some are good and some are full of hype. The essence though is that our thoughts create our world. So if we focus on not enough money and if we are constantly worried about debt, we stay stuck in a mountain of debt. If we focus on getting better with managing our money, seeing ourselves getting that promotion, or visualizing paying off the car loan, the energy shifts and good starts flowing our way.

"Every thought we think is creating our future." ~ Louise Hays

If you want a simple life, but one filled with meaning, it's important to understand what we feel we deserve. It affects how we deal with money, what we spend and why. To be able to live a simpler life, we still need to deal with current real-world money issues and debt. So we will discuss some basics on how to deal with money. I encourage you, though, to take the time to really think about this first section on your underlying views of worthiness.

Money, Money, Money

Money is the single most common source of stress for the largest number of people. It can drive a wedge between couples and in families. Many trapped by money problems feel they are victims. Sleepless nights become common since your brain is working overtime to figure out how to pay the electric bill.

Are you like Ann? She's overworked, tired and frustrated and on the weekends she shops to give herself a little treat -- like a reprieve from anxiety. She does this over and over again, and soon she has created another layer of stress with unmanageable credit card debt.

Or are you more like Victoria? She does a good job of sticking to her family's monthly budget...until the holidays roll around. She was planning on buying five ten dollar stocking stuffers for friends at the office. Once she got to the mall, Victoria got caught up in the holiday spirit, saw so many cute items, and spent hundreds of dollars on extra gifts.

It doesn't matter if you consistently buy items you don't really need, or you go overboard for a holiday, birthday, or anniversary. You have spent more than you planned, and that causes more stress. Now you need to work even harder to pay for those purchases.

Simplify Cash Flow

There are no two ways about it. If you're spending more than you're earning, you have a negative cash flow. Whether you owe a parent, friends, the credit card company, the car company, or the bank, you cannot save regularly for your future. You feel that setting a budget is too rigid and restrictive. You don't balance your checkbooks because it is just not something you are good at. (Or is it really because you don't want to know how much you are spending?)

This is not to suggest that you do a radical, massive overhaul, and completely stop all spending on everything that is not truly a necessity.   That can work and may be the solution for some people. For most, it's not doable long-term.

What is necessary is that you begin taking responsibility for what is being spent and know, really know, where your money is going. If you are not good at this, then have someone else help you. A spouse, a good friend, a trusted bookkeeper – find someone who will give you the basic information to help you understand where you are at financially at this moment.

Here's a really simple exercise, which can be a lot of fun. Look at it as a short trip into self-discovery, rather than as a boring, must-do assignment. Carry a little notebook around with you or create lists in your smartphone. Promise yourself that you will do this exercise thoroughly for one week.

Divide your expenses for the week into these categories:

Essentials – Food, rent, gas, public transportation, utilities, gym/yoga, personal care items, such as toothpaste, soap, paper products, etc.

Little Luxuries – Your morning Starbucks coffee, after-work cocktails, eating out, new make-up, expensive shampoos, haircuts, movie tickets, iTunes downloads, Amazon books, etc.

Big Luxuries – Hair highlights, the latest new cell phone on the market, the new spring handbags, designer shoes, a two-week trip to Hawaii, etc.

These are not hard and fast definitions. You can come up with your own categories. The important part is to jot down EVERY expense for one week. Don't analyze, just write everything down. After the week is done, then go back and review. That will give you a sense of how you spend your money.

Make it even more fun by creating a Pinterest collage at the end of the week to visually depict where your money is going. Definitely far more fun than drawing up a boring budget, but you still get the picture!

Here's the next step of the challenge. Create another column or another section on your collage entitled "Savings." Note the purchases that you could have skipped during the week, such as your eating out for the fifth night in a row. In this example, move the amount you spent eating out into the "Savings" column.

You've heard it hundreds of times before but skipping your morning stop at your local coffee shop can save you a pretty penny. Savings advice is dull, but when you can actually see how much you can save and find an easy way to do that, it becomes much more interesting and rewarding. If it's more interesting, you are more likely to make the changes necessary.

If a paper notebook is as extinct to you as the dodo bird, there are some really fun smartphone apps to simplify your spending and to figure out how much you can save. "Savings Calculator" is a free, simple, and easy to manage app that calculates how much you can save over a period of time – week/month/half year by forsaking certain expenditures.

You could start with simple questions like, "How much would I save if I skipped my afternoon latte for 2 months?" or "How much can I save if I reduce eating out to twice a week for four months." It is really a flash calculator and doesn't take into account compounding interest, but when you realize that you can save $9,125 a year by setting aside $25 every day and $18,250 for two years, that should spur you into making some positive changes.

"All prosperity begins in the mind and is dependent only on the full use of our creative imagination." ~Ruth Ross

When you see how easy it is to eliminate your debt and to start building wealth by making small, simple changes, you'll be inspired to take even more steps in the right direction. These are really small steps but carried out consciously and consistently, on a daily basis, the returns in the form of increased self-esteem, sense of financial freedom and independence are priceless!

What Does Your Debt Cost?

The typical person has loans, credit cards, and overdrafts. Each lending company has its own lending rates and payment cycles, so it can be tricky to stay on top of all of them. Making the minimum monthly payments on credit card bills does not lead to financial freedom. Learning the length of time it would take to pay off a credit card balance by only paying the minimum due is worse than shock therapy!

Here are some hard, cold figures. Say you have $5,000 owing on a credit card which charges 19.9% interest. If you pay $100 a month, it will take you 107 months (a little short of 9 years) to completely pay it off. And that's only one credit card. Many of us have at least three or four. If we were to pay off these cards in a linear fashion, i.e., pay one down and pay off the next (it doesn't work like that in the real world but let's play along for now), it would take roughly 36 years to completely pay off $20,000 in debt. That's half the life span for many of us and it's far too long to spend shackled to debt.

Fortunately, technology today has many apps to make our lives easier. "Debt Payoff Planner" is an Android app which helps users get a better grip on their debt by figuring out which ones should be paid off first, how many payments are left before you get to a zero balance, and number of days left before you fully erase those debts. For less than $1.00, you get graphs and payment plan suggestions.

iPhone users have a number of options such as "Debt Free-Pay Off Your Debt with Debt Snowball method or Debt Snowball+." Like most other apps, "Debt Snowball+" will calculate how much time is required to pay off the debt with just minimum payments. However, you can tweak the calculation and figure out how much faster you arrive at that desired point just by paying an extra sum of money every month.

In the end, the apps are just tools. Addressing the mounting debts is much easier when you realize that you actually have control, either by cutting back on some expenses and applying it to the debt, or by just being fully aware of how to manage your finances.

If you approach managing your money like a game, as opposed to a tedious exercise, the apps and your playful attitude will take the tedium out of responsible debt management.

Raising Funds Easily and Simply

After reading that, you may be thinking, "Well, I wanted to start my own business, but I don't know if it's wise to do that now." Starting a new business has many benefits. If you truly want to create a life that you love, doing work that's meaningful to you is a key element, but there are always initial expenses.

The costs vary depending on if you are starting a local retail store or service, or starting an online business. Even if your business is low cost, in today's world it's necessary to have a website, business cards, and some marketing materials. Every person's situation is unique so no one except you can truly evaluate if now is the right time to launch your business. Look at your situation, your energy level, what support you have, and what resources are available to you.

If you decide that now is the time to start living your dream, you may have set aside savings to finance your life during the gestation period of the business, but what if the money doesn't stretch far enough? How do you raise funds in a simple and easy fashion?

The traditional method was to set up an appointment with the bank manager, prepare a business plan (and how many of us know how to do that?) and make a case for a loan. Getting a loan today for a new business is extremely difficult, if not impossible. So what are some other options?

(Note: if funding your dream isn't one of your priorities today, skip this section and go to the end of this chapter for Today's STRUT ideas. You can always come back later for this info, or pass this on to a friend or family member who is exploring ways to fund a project or business idea.)

Simple, Potent Funding Possibilities

You don't have to leave your dream behind because the bank manager doesn't share your vision. Crowdfunding has become the way for many solid creative projects and businesses to take off, without the yoke of high interest payments. So you can still create your simple life with your dream business, without the pressures of traditional loans.

Basically, crowdfunding is exactly what it sounds like. You get money from a crowd of individuals or backers. It is a form of micro-patronage. Pledges can start as low as $1.00 each (getting 100,000 people to donate $1.00 each gets you a rather nice sum of money). You set the terms for each category of donation or pledge and you give a little reward in return. It could be as small as a button or as large as a crate of 100 watches, as in the case of Pebble Technology.

Pebble Technology was operating out of crammed split-level condo in Palo Alto, California, but has now become the poster child of crowdfunding success. Its founder, then 26-year-old Eric Migicovsky, designed a "smart" wristwatch that connects wirelessly to the Android and iPhones. It is a companion to the smartphones and is customized to the needs of the wearer who can download new watch faces, get sports and fitness apps, as well as notifications sent from the smartphone.

He started with a prototype built from cell phone parts. The company needed $100,000 and turned to Kickstarter. It created pledge categories from $99 for a Jet Black Pebble Watch to $1,250 per pledge in return for a custom watch face designed to your specifications.

Within 28 hours, Pebble had raised more $1 million from backers who were each willing to pledge $115 to pre-order the watches. (The retail price of the watches was to be $155.) Within a month, Pebble had snagged $10.27 million from nearly 69,000 clients, setting records for the largest amount of funds raised via crowdfunding.

There are all sorts of projects that have successfully raised money on the crowdfunding sites. You may have a simple idea such as creating a photo book on dogs, writing a children's book, growing a rooftop garden to promote sustainability, putting together a record of harpsichord music. Maybe you may want to raise funds to start a vegan bakery.

The success of your project depends on how unique it is, how you describe it on the crowdfunding websites and what you return to the pledgers.

Again, these are all tools. The key here is to recognize that there are many options that maybe you aren't even aware of. Getting funds to create a dream project is no longer just a pipe-dream.

Of course, it all begins within, to recognize that you are the one responsible for your money health, and when you step up to the plate, life rises up to meet you. For more details on crowdfunding sites, see the "Resources" section.

Today's STRUT
(Simple Tips for your Remarkable Unique Transformation)

Changing your Money Patterns

1. Think of one small way that you can shift your attitude toward money. You could go to the library or buy a book on positive thinking or prosperity consciousness to learn more.

2. Identify two expenses of $10 or less which you spend frequently but which fall into the "small luxuries" category. Skip these two expenses for a week (or better yet, a month) and direct the money into a savings account.

3. Use the savings at the end of this period to make an additional payment on your highest interest credit card debt.

4. Do a special "A-bun-dance" dance when you have tackled one money issue. Celebrate and make it fun. Congratulate yourself when you have small wins to create a simpler life by lessening your money worries.

Affirmations:

I attract all the money I need to more than take care of my needs and debt.
Every step I take moves me towards financial freedom.
I value my time and energy and manage my money wisely and responsibly.

A Little Help From Your Friends

Real-Life RUST
(Routines that Undermine your Simple living Techniques)
- You don't want to burden your friends. You can handle the problem yourself.
- You have to spend your time working. You'll get together with friends next month.
- You are married so you feel your spouse is the only support person you need.

Simply by:
- Making time to connect with friends and family that are important to you.
- Dropping the mask. Being vulnerable and sharing what's happening in your life.
- Being your best supporter. Taking care of yourself, so you can be there for those that matter.

"Of all the music that reached farthest into heaven, it is the beating of a loving heart." ~Henry Beecher Stowe

Mary is new in San Francisco and thrilled about her job as a software programmer in Silicon Valley. There is unlimited potential for her there and she plunges into her work with gusto. As an employee in a new start-up, she has long days at work turning into long nights in order to meet urgent deadlines.

Four months later, she has yet to make a friend in her community. Worried about losing her job at a time when great jobs are at a premium, she's turned down numerous invitations from colleagues in her department to go out for drinks.

When she badly sprains her ankle over the weekend and is confined to bed, she is startled when she realizes that she has no close friends in that city to turn to for help. There's no trusted friend she can count on to shop for her groceries for the week, or to help with the mountain of laundry which needs to get done for the following week.

Sadly, she feels she could be on her deathbed, and no one would notice her absence. Her colleagues and bosses would only be curious about her welfare after she failed to be at work on time on Monday.

Mary learned the hard way the importance of investing energy into building a support system. She felt a deep loneliness which will continue to worsen until she learns to reach out. If she does not put this on her priority list, she will find herself tired, lonely and miserable once the glamour of the new job wears off.

Finding your Support System

Who are the people who make up your support system? If you're married or are involved in a relationship, your main support may come from your significant other. Your support system can also be your parents and your siblings.

In this highly mobile society if you live far away from your roots, your support probably comes from your friends at work, school, church, or social groups. Your pets are also part of your support system. Who better than to lighten your mood after a tough day at work than your best four-legged pal!

Children can also be a source of support. They may seem to be the ones needing support, but their unquestioning love and innocent joy of life pulls us to fully enjoy the moment.

Picture your life as a jig-saw puzzle that is to be pieced together. Your support system is the focal point in the center without which the picture is incomplete.

In this stress-fuelled society, we need emotional anchors to avoid feeling adrift, unwanted and alone. Without a support system, we begin to feel that there's a gaping hole in our chest that professional success and a profitable business cannot fill.

The key is to know how to ask for support and how to be grateful for the support you receive. It's vitally important to remember to invest time and energy to nurture this support team. Make sure that work doesn't steamroll over these important relationships. Commit time to keeping the relationships fresh, positive and energized.

Experience shows that people who develop and have a support system in place are:

- Encouraged to make changes to improve their lives
- More likely to step out of their comfort zone
- Held accountable to follow through
- More disciplined and more likely to succeed
- Finding hope from unexpected sources
- Generally happier

Here are some examples of how you can create a support system:

- Stay-at-home moms who create a car pool to take turns ferrying their children to and from school. (This seems like such an obvious thing to do, but many moms are too shy or too consumed with work to ask for help.)

- Pet owners in a condo complex take turns walking each other's pets or take over the feeding of a pet when an owner is out-of-town.

- A work group to brainstorm and exchange ideas on how to start a green business. Everyone benefits from the group mind.

- A group of city residents getting together to turn an urban junkyard into a sustainable garden for growing their own food.

- Enlisting Divine support in good times and in difficult times. We are not accidents of biological soup. There is a Great Architect at work.

Know How to Ask for Help

Some of you prefer to withdraw and go it alone when the going gets tough. You develop a hard shell, the walls go right up and you become uncommunicative. You're behaving almost as if you're the only person who has the answers to the problem and you are the only one who knows the "right way" of finding the solution.

Others shy away from asking for help for fear of looking vulnerable, or being afraid that they are imposing on others. If you are afraid of rejection, you may reject the people around you first.

If you don't speak up and ask for help, the people around you may be oblivious to your needs. If you need a new job, brainstorm with the people in your life on how to find new opportunities. Get the word out to friends and neighbors and through social media.

When you ask, do so with the confidence that life is listening. Be clear and specific. Ask in love and gratitude, not in desperation and fear. You'll be surprised what doors open up for you when you make the move to ask.

Remember that it is ok to ask for help. None of us has all the answers, and life has its ups and downs. We all need help from others at many points in our lives.

Reduce stress by getting friends and family on board. Get the kids to put their own toys away rather than attempting to be Super-Mom. Make a request of your partner to handle the cooking a couple of nights a week.

If you have a busy travel schedule, plan ahead for get-togethers with your friends in the city you'll be visiting so you can maximize your time with them during your trip. Share your schedule with them, so they understand when you are available and when you have other commitments.

In addition to asking for help, remember to offer your help to friends and family whenever you can. If someone is having a tough time with her teenager, lend a listening ear or invite her to do something fun. When you can give back to your friends and family, it's easier for many to ask when they need some help.

When a Relationship Ends

If a partner in a relationship continually makes positive changes and outgrows the other, the one left behind is likely to feel resentful and may call it quits. If you were in this situation, do you hang on in the hope that your partner will come around to your point of view and change?

You can only control your own path. As you focus on your own development, you can hope but not insist that your loved ones will travel the same journey. Sometimes, paths will diverge despite the best of intentions on the part of both parties. By hanging on to a relationship that has outlived its purpose, you are taking on more stress and, in fact, jeopardizing your own journey because you then begin to carry the weight of two people on your shoulders.

You're also laying the guilt trip on your partner by hoping that he or she will change and come around to your way of thinking. Such expectations drive a bigger wedge through a relationship and accelerate its end, probably with big drama and tears, at a faster rate than if it were allowed to run its course amicably.

You can forsake the burden of trying to force change by recognizing that we each have our own path to walk, and we can't force another to accompany us. All we can do is focus on our own steps and hope that we will inspire others to follow along by example.

Other than the death of a loved one, saying goodbye to a relationship that was rich in potential is one of the hardest and most difficult experiences to endure. It's heart-wrenching. To many, it seems safer to stay stuck in the past, and ignore the possibilities of the future. You can choose to muddle your growth by living in the past and fantasizing about a future that will not happen, or you can cut loose and move on.

There are a few things you can do to simplify the process of grieving and moving on:

- Reach out to your support group or community. Find one or two friends with whom you feel safe in exposing your feelings. Having a few friends you can count on, to sit and eat popcorn with while watching a movie, or to talk to when you cannot sleep at night makes a world of difference.

- Alternatively, you may be more comfortable with a circle of people who are going through similar experiences by joining a grief-counseling group. You may find that you are not as alone on this leg of the journey as you may have initially thought. This may even help you move through your grieving faster.

- Find the lesson in the loss to heal faster. Understanding what happened will allow you to apply the lesson to a future relationship.

Every ending contains the seed for a new beginning. It's important to understand that the seed cannot blossom into a fresh opportunity if you hold on so tightly to the past that the seed can't open up and grow. Be open to the lesson and let the new chance for personal growth take root.

Simplify your life by shedding the baggage of lost relationships. Be gentle with yourself during the grieving process, but be assured that in time, you'll be facing the future with renewed hope and greater self-knowledge to guide you to making better relationship choices.

Be Your #1 Supporter

Are you your own worst critic? Are you still harsh on yourself for mistakes you made a year ago or decades ago? Have you forgiven yourself for not seeing the breakup or the job loss coming?

If you're finding life difficult and hard to handle, check in to see if you are chained to unwanted regrets and anger over past mistakes. If you're still shackled to a ball and chain, how do you expect to move on to new and fresh experiences?

We should be our own best supporter, our own cheerleading team of one, because if we don't support ourselves, how can we expect others to support us? Take some time to look inward to see where the weight of regret is residing.

What are you still beating yourself up about? Common examples are:

- Not saving enough money when you were working several jobs
- Burning the candle at both ends and ignoring the needs of your body

- Dropping out of your university program
- Playing it safe by taking the job that paid more money rather than following the job that fueled your passion
- Waiting too long to start a family or
- Wishing you would have pursued a career before starting a family so young

These questions will help you to cast a fresh perspective on your past choices.

- Given the information you had then, could you have made a different decision? (Usually every one of us does the best we can with the information we had at the time. When we learn more, we make better choices.)
- Were you making the decision alone or were you being supported by loving friends and family who offered guidance?
- Have you learned from the lesson and benefited from the new self-knowledge?

Life is one big grand adventure, just like a roller coaster. It's much more fun when you have companions along the way. A smart support system is one of the necessary pillars in the foundation that supports your life.

****

Today's STRUT *(Simple Tips for your Remarkable Unique Transformation)*

Shoulders to Lean On

1. Find a support group in your local area. Even if you are not ready to emotionally share with a group of strangers, you can take first steps by joining a group with some of your interests, such as Golden Lab pet owners' group, a mystery book club, or an outdoors group with interests in hiking and canoeing.

2. Send a friend a card in the mail. Hardly anyone does that anymore and this act of thoughtfulness opens a door for more communication. Schedule a lunch date and start nurturing that relationship.
   12.
3. Ask for help when you are going through a difficult time. Don't wallow in your difficulties, but if you need help, ask. Then when you are stronger, be attentive to your friends' needs and be there when they need a shoulder.

Affirmations:

I easily find my way to a support group that appreciates me for who I am.
I am deeply grateful for the constant support of my family, my friends, my co-workers and my bosses.
My courage supports me to live my life by my rules, and on my terms.

Have Fun!

Real-Life RUST *(Routines that Undermine Simple living Techniques)*
- You work constantly and feel that you don't have any time for fun
- You take life way too seriously
- You can't laugh at yourself or your mistakes

Simplify by:
- Remembering what you did for fun as a kid and do that very thing (or something similar)
- Scheduling in some time for fun activities every week
- Laughing whenever possible -- at Jeff Dunham DVDs, with family over silly things you did as a child, or at funny videos on You Tube

"Don't stop having fun when you get older because you will get older when you stop having fun." ~Author Unknown

All of us have busy lives. We are starved of time to get everything that needs doing done. More than likely, we are not creating enough room for fun. You have been working on creating more balance and simplifying your life. Now it's time to address having some fun.

Sue was coming to the end of her rope. In her late 40's, she was juggling many responsibilities. Her aging father was suffering from dementia and had to be admitted into a care facility. Her oldest daughter in high school was hanging out with what Sue termed "the wrong crowd," experimenting with drugs and alcohol, and neglecting her school work. Sue was the office manager of a small local chain of packing supply stores. Her boss had been hospitalized for a heart attack so he was relying on Sue to keep the business afloat.

When Sue turned to a coach for help, it wasn't to get emotional support or for help in dealing with her family problems. Instead, it was to relearn how to have fun again. As Sue put it, "I have been a caregiver for so long, I don't know how to laugh anymore."

Sue recognized that her life was seriously out of balance. However, she intuitively grasped that if she got in touch with her silly side, she would be able to gain a fresh perspective on her life. She knew that somehow she needed (and wanted) to be reminded how to laugh so loud she would have a belly-ache.

If she could laugh again, then perhaps she would not see her family and work responsibilities as being so burdensome. The task before her was to get in touch with what brings her pleasure, and how to identify those activities that would allow her to feel joy again.

Most of us probably can relate to Sue's quest. Yet, sometimes some of us take fun to the extreme. Marci packed every spare moment with "fun" activities. She was always searching for the latest and greatest activities. She explored self-help workshops, networking groups, book club meetings, quilting parties, cooking classes, painting classes, Pilates, kayaking, scrapbooking, paddle-boarding, rescuing lost dogs and cats, and her list went on and on.

Marci equated activities with fun. She grew up with parents that worked constantly, and Marci vowed she would not follow in those footsteps. She felt she always had to be doing something and be involved in the latest fad to stay hip and popular.

She kept an insane schedule until she got really sick. Her constant non-stop schedule over the past year had caused serious fatigue, among other health issues. She was forced to stop and get well. It was only then that she began to realize there is a happy medium between not making any time for fun activities, and becoming obsessed with being at the center of every new event.

Fun makes us feel good. We forget our challenges and we're reminded of the childish innocence we had during the first 10 years of our lives (until we started growing up far too quickly).

To simplify our life, we often forget that sometimes the most fun we can have is right before us. It's the simple things like watching a silly reality TV show with some of our best girlfriends, or watching our dogs chase leaves while taking a walk. It can be cuddling up with our partner in front of the fireplace with a cup of delicious, steaming hot chocolate, or making fools of ourselves playing charades with friends.

In the rush to have fun, we've forgotten the essence of what fun truly means. While rolling-on-the-floor laughing is wonderful, that's not the only definition of fun. It could be as simple as catching up on the latest novel while having a pedicure.

Fun is something that brings lightness and pleasure. It is being able to wholly absorb the experience of the moment, to fully engage all the senses in what you are doing at that point in time.

Fun – Getting Back to Basics

One way of simply having fun is to get back to basics. Ask yourself what truly makes you laugh. Which memories do you recall as, "I was really having fun then." For many of us, it's easiest to think back to our childhood days, back to when the world was golden and we had no heavy responsibilities resting on our shoulders.

"Unless each day can be looked back upon by an individual as one in which he has had some fun, some joy, some real satisfaction, that day is a loss." ~Author Unknown

As kids, making mud pies or sandcastles on the beach were fun. Being doused by the water sprinkler on hot days, jumping into the swimming pool, riding the merry-go-round in the carnival, going to the circus, simply hanging around with our friends -- those were fun-filled days.

This is not just a trip into nostalgia. By getting in touch with our childhood, we can find clues to whatever it is that can bring us joy as adults in today's world. By remembering our best moments as kids, we can once again find inspiration to help us balance our lives.

Here is a simple exercise. Jot down five to seven activities that you loved to do as a kid and label that as "Fun Then." Now write down activities that are similar that you could do now and label that as "Fun Now." Your list might look something like this:

Fun Then: Swimming
Fun Now: Paddle-boarding or scuba diving

Fun Then: Painting
Fun Now: Painting classes, volunteering at an art museum

Fun Then: Board games
Fun Now: Pictionary or online Scrabble

Fun Then: Acting in school plays
Fun Now: Improv comedy classes or attending local plays

Fun Then: Dancing
Fun Now: Salsa or ballroom dance classes; Zumba classes

Fun Then: Just hanging around
Fun Now: Lunch with friends; weekly manicures

Fun Then: Reading
Fun Now: Joining a book club

From this, you should glean that you could make room in your calendar for dancing classes. If you are already taking a scrapbooking class, but really now connect with the joy you felt from dancing, make some changes. Do what brings you the most "fun" or enjoyment.

Some activities don't require a lot of planning or any long-term commitment. Get a few friends together for a game of Pictionary, or to play online scrabble with a friend across the country. Maybe you have no time for formal dancing classes, but enrolling in a Zumba class gives you the best of both worlds -- dance moves plus exercise to keep you in shape.

It's rather amazing what you can learn from your childhood self. Plus, a list like this helps you get refocused on your priorities. What is important is that you make time for fun activities now, rather than waiting for a perfect time. (We all know that there is never a perfect time.)

If regular reading seems a little boring to you, turn it into a fun activity by attending a book club event, or going with a girlfriend to the local library. Check out which well-known author is coming to your city to speak. By participating in events like this, you may have an opportunity to get tips from a published author and insights into the creative world of writing.

Think outside the box when it comes to having fun. Ask your friends for ideas and then make sure that you have some down-time regularly. Your body, mind, and soul all need time for fun.

Fun Opens Doors

There's no telling what doors life will open up for you when you have fun. Mallory, a cellist with an orchestra, came up with a list rather similar to our example. She loved to travel, enjoyed learning new languages and immersing herself in new cultures. She was single and she was getting tired of travelling alone, eating by herself in restaurants and not having anyone to share the experiences with.

In her list, Mallory gave a high priority to dancing classes because the music and the movement would energize her. When she had the occasional dance class, she was thrilled because it opened up something inside of her.

She decided that for her next vacation she would sign up for samba classes -- in Brazil. She conducted research online and found samba classes for beginners. The school that caught her eye also offered Portuguese classes that would improve her speaking, understanding, reading, and writing of that new language. For a small extra fee, she also signed up for capoeira, a Brazilian martial arts discipline that fuses both music and dance.

Mallory was in heaven during her vacation. She made many new friends, most of whom had travelled in from other countries for this unique package. She never had to eat out alone during this vacation. She fulfilled a long-held dream to master samba steps so she would no longer feel like a wallflower at parties.

Additionally and unexpectedly, the confidence she gained in her body movements from both samba and capoeira endowed her music with a passion she had never felt before. It was as if she were no longer playing from her head and relying on her intellect to interpret the music sheets.

Instead, Mallory felt her whole body engaging when she played her cello. Her new found passion made her performances so exciting that she caught the eye of a concert promoter who was looking for someone to join the global troupe for a world-renowned singer. Doors to new experiences, new fun, new people and a brand new career opened up when she followed her heart and had fun.

Is it any wonder that "Gangnam Style" went gangbusters and broke records, such as being the only video to have more than a billion views on You Tube, setting the record within six months of its release? The video by South Korean rapper, Psy, has spawned parodies by members of the British army in Afghanistan, the U.S. Navy, inmates in a Filipino prison, and countless other copycats around the world.

Although originally designed to be a satire on a wealthy South Korean suburb, "Gangnam Style" took the world by storm because of the catchy music and the equally catchy dance moves, put together by a guy who simply went out to have a whole lot of fun.

In various interviews, Psy quoted that everyone on the set was "crying from laughing" because they were having so much fun with the production. Psy uploaded the video for his South Korean fans, without realizing that through that upload, he would end up being world famous.

He was later invited to be on the Ellen DeGeneres show, to sing with Britney Spears, and to perform in front of U.S. President, Barack Obama. Not bad for a pop star who was only previously known in South Korea.

Lighten Up Within

Apollinaire, a French author, hit the nail on the head when he advised that now and again, we should pause and just be happy. You would think he was making a commentary about our lives in the modern world, but Apollinaire was a French playwright and poet who died in 1918.

"Now and then it's good to pause in our pursuit of happiness and just be happy." ~Guillaume Apollinaire

Man's pursuit of happiness transcends time and space. As we awaken to consciousness, we become more aware that, even as time seems to be accelerating, we can get more out of each minute by changing our inner dialogue and by lightening up from within.

On any given day, each of us has about 60,000 thoughts. How many of yours are focused on what can go right rather than what can go wrong? Maybe the primitive parts of our brains are still wired to those times when taking a walk in the woods would expose us to predators or enemy warriors. But we live in a modern world where we have more opportunity than our ancestors, and more awareness that we do control our lives by controlling our thoughts.

We can make our lives more complete by simply filling our thoughts with more humor, by finding something funny in our daily routine, and by laughing at ourselves. Yes, especially laughing at our mistakes. If we don't laugh at our mistakes, how are we going to learn and find a better way? If we don't shrug off our regrets by having a good laugh about our silliness, we can get trapped in the past.

Laughing at our foibles releases our creativity and encourages us to step outside our comfort zone. It encourages us to try again, to find new ways to tap our potential, to release fears and live life fully.

Look at the clown in the circus. He falls over himself walking on boots that are ten sizes too big. He wears mismatched clothes with a hole in the back of his pants, and he has a red nose. Yet, both kids and adults adore him, because he allows himself to be silly and he mirrors that secret wish inside us to have the courage to be free to laugh at our mistakes.

Today, release your inner clown. Go for it! For a few minutes stop taking life so seriously. When you make a mistake, shake it off, laugh about it, and move on.

Today's STRUT *(Simple Tips for your Remarkable Unique Transformation)*

Laugh and Enjoy Today

1. What is one fun activity you would love to do? Don't let the reasons why you can't do that flood in. Think of one thing you really want to do. Check out how you can do that? Go online, call a friend, or check the local events calendar for classes or activities. Then DO IT!

2. Write a couple of sentences about how liberating that activity felt. Post that where you are reminded of that feeling every day. Or better yet, take a photo of you doing that activity and upload it as a screen saver on your computer.

3. Now schedule time to do that activity again, or find another new activity to experience. Get in the habit of doing something fun regularly.

4. Find something to laugh about every day!

Affirmations:

I find something amusing to laugh about every day.
The simplest things bring a smile to my face.
I am grateful for the fun activities and people in my life.

Simplify from the Inside Out

Bottom line: To have the simple life you dream of, you must start being the person you were created to be. If you start trusting that you do know what's best for you, and act from that wisdom, then the struggles and pressures lessen. This takes practice, but you will soon see that there's a difference in your decisions, your choices, your conversations with others, and your purchases. Your outer world will begin reflecting what is in your heart and what's important to you. That congruity brings more peace and joy in everyday life. And when you have that, life becomes much simpler.

The various ways to make the important internal shifts that were discussed in the book are listed below. Which was most helpful?

- **Visualizing and creating what you want your life to look like**

- **Identifying your core values to know what's truly important**

- **Learning how to set boundaries and how to say "no"**

- **Tuning in to your inner wisdom for guidance**

- **Being grateful for everything (little or big, good or not so good)**

- **Using time more effectively by setting priorities**

- **Finding out how to bring more of YOU into your work**

- **Seeing money differently and learning ideas for money management**

- **Learning to ask for help**

- **Celebrating and having fun**

- **Knowing you now have ideas on how to create a simpler, happier life**

For more information, visit http://DonnaJDavis.com

Resources

In Money and Abundance, options for raising money for your dream were mentioned. Below are various crowdfunding sites. Check out their website for more details on structure, fees, and features.

Simple Guide to Crowdfunding Sites

1. Kickstarter www.kickstarter.com is the most popular crowdfunding site and accepts creative projects.

2. Indiegogo www.indiegogo.com is similar to Kickstarter and accepts any project including charitable and non-profit causes.

3. RocketHub www.rockethub.com presents opportunities, through contests, for creatives to work with top-notch labels, world-class publicists and companies to raise public awareness of their talents.

4. GoFundMe www.gofundme.com helps you raise money for a cause, even for personal needs. Money can be raised to pay your pet's medical bills or even for funerals, memorials or ice-hockey classes.

5. Razoo www.razoo.com raises money for worthy causes in four main categories: nonprofits, individuals, companies and foundations. Under-budgeted elementary schools and a religious community that provides housing and care for mentally disabled individuals have raised funds through this site.

6. Crowdrise www.crowdrise.com raises money for real world issues. They fund animal welfare, relief programs, education, and even some personal projects.

7. PledgeMusic www.pledgemusic.com is a hands-on site reaching out to music fans to bring new talent into the industry.

8. SellaBand www.sellaband.com has been reinvented and now allows music artists to strike any deal with any music label or promotion company.

9. Appbackr www.appbackr.com funds projects for mobile apps.

10. Crowdfunder www.crowdfunder.com is slightly different and has angel investors for various projects in exchange for some portion of equity in the business.

About the Author

Donna J. Davis is a business consultant and author. She owns and runs Next Level Accounting, Inc. and DJD Communications, LLC in Tucson, AZ.

She is passionate about helping others reconnect with their dreams and create a simple life filled with joy and meaning.

Learn more at http://DonnaJDavis.com.

Review Request

Thank you for reading. I hope you found several ways that will help you start simplifying your life to reduce the stress you're facing.

Many people look at the reviews on Amazon before they decide to purchase a book. If you liked the book, **would you please take a minute** to leave a review with your feedback?

You can review my book by logging back into Amazon. Scroll down past the current reviews. You will see a box that says "Write a customer review." I would very much appreciate it if you would tell others something you liked in the book.

If there is anything you did not like, please email me directly at djdcommunications@gmail.com. I do read these and will use your comments to make future versions better. Thank you so much!

Donna J. Davis

Notes and Favorite Ideas

27324963R00070

Made in the USA
Lexington, KY
04 November 2013